The Drovers are Coming to Morpeth Town

CW00553043

Bridget Gubbins

with original illustrations by Victor Ambrus

Published by
Greater Morpeth Development Trust

**Greater Morpeth
Development Trust**
Regeneration of town & countryside
www.gmdt.net

Published by:
Greater Morpeth Development Trust
Carlisle Park Lodge
Castle Square
Morpeth
Northumberland
NE61 1YD

First published 2012

© Bridget Gubbins

The right of Bridget Gubbins to be identified as the author of this work has been asserted by her in accordance with the Copyrights, Designs and Patents Act 1988.

British Library Cataloguing in Publication Data
A catalogue reference for this book is available from the British Library.

ISBN 978-0-9568683-1-2

Original illustrations © Victor Ambrus

Front cover illustration by Victor Ambrus
Back cover map by Azure Printing

Printed in Great Britain by Martins the Printers Ltd, Sea View Works, Spittal, Berwick upon Tweed, TD15 1RS

Contents

Preface

Preface

"That's a holloway leading down from the ramparts," said the archaeologist. We were on a group walk at one of Northumberland's hillforts. "What's that? Isn't it the name of a prison in London?" I asked. He explained that it was a hollowed out pathway made by the movements of animals, and that this went on over the centuries. The London name would have described a similar route. He said there were lots of them in this area, and waved vaguely over the heather. "They were drove roads leading to Morpeth."

At around the same time, a new book was coming out, *Drove Roads of Northumberland*. I bought it and read it greedily, and soon followed that with two other classic books on the subject, *The Drove Roads of Scotland* and *The Drovers*. I was captivated.

A springtime of reading and research, and a summer of tracking the routes to Morpeth from Scotland, were next. What was it like to be a drover? Where did they come from? How did they know the way? This story is the result; part history, part exploration.

I had to remember all the time that the animals were being driven to the market, ultimately to be killed for food. Once at Morpeth, some would be sold on for breeding or further fattening, but for many, the butchers' shops were their final destination.

Maps

Northumberland Archives, at Woodhorn Museum near Ashington, is the place to go for old maps. I've mainly used the Armstrong maps of 1769, Fryer maps of 1820, Greenwood maps of 1828 and the first edition Ordnance Survey maps of the 1860s. I've included examples of each in the text, so readers can get a sense of the different formats. They are all easily accessible in drawers and on shelves near the reception desk at Woodhorn. There are many, many more old routes waiting to be identified and explored.

The routes I've chosen in three of the chapters are shown in simplified form in the appendix. They can be followed in more detail on OS maps below, or the equivalent Explorer maps.

> Chapter 3 – Landranger 74, 75, 81
> Chapter 5 – Landranger 74, 80, 81
> Chapter 7 – Landranger 80, 81

The routes are linear, following the way the drovers came with their herds and flocks from the north. I would find a way to get to the starting point, and then head for Morpeth. Walkers and cyclists will understand the logistics of linear walking. Armchair travellers can sit back and not worry about it.

The routes I've chosen lead towards Morpeth from the north, in a southerly or south-easterly direction. The descriptions and the photos follow those directions in almost all cases, so you can start with me, and look towards your destination all the time.

Old Bakehouse Yard, Morpeth, 2012   Bridget Gubbins

Acknowledgments
Greater Morpeth Development Trust, Liz Young, management and advice
John Griffiths, Kim Bibby-Wilson, John Bibby, reading and historical advice
Keith Gilroy, Northumberland Archives, design and historical advice
John McErlane and David Brookes, rights of way advice
Bailiffgate Museum, access to their newspaper archives
Doug McPhail and Colin Harvey, footpaths advice
Susan Rogers, information and advice
Harry Beamish and Lloyd Langley, National Trust at Wallington, advice and access to maps
Scottish Borders Council staff, re-setting fallen milestone
Butchers, shepherds, farmers, drovers, foresters, archaeologists, patiently answering questions
Mary Harris, an indomitable drove-road companion

Extract from the 1686 petition to Parliament, by landowners from Morpeth, requesting the renewal of an Act of Parliament to control the "Multitudes of Scotch Cattell and Sheep which weekely cloy our Marketts". Animals brought to Morpeth by Scottish drovers were depressing the prices for local farmers.

Reproduced with permission of Northumberland Archives

1   The drovers are coming to Morpeth town   1686 - 1910

The Highlanders are approaching the streets of Morpeth. People going about their daily affairs on this day in 1686 become aware of the *hoo hoo* cry as the drovers direct their shaggy black cattle forward. They hear the lowing of the animals and the clattering of hooves on the cobblestones, and sniff the pungent beasts as they approach from the north down Newgate Street. Some of the drovers pause for a refreshing tankard, or a bite of bread and cheese, using English awkwardly, and when they turn to each other they speak their strange soft Gaelic language. Local lasses peep at the foreign lads wearing their swinging, gathered kilts, the plaid thrown stylishly over the shoulder.

Sometimes, the drovers would pass through the market place, and over the bridge towards Newcastle, where they were heading for the great August or October fairs[1], or towards the fattening fields of southern cities. At other times, they pastured the cattle in fields near the River Wansbeck, resting them overnight before Morpeth's weekly market.

The Highland drovers had been passing this way over hundreds of years, and during the second half of the seventeenth century they were coming more and more frequently.

Morpeth is a meat town. Throughout history, animals have been driven here, on the hoof, and for many of them it was their final journey. Others walked on further, to Newcastle, North Shields, Yorkshire, even as far as London, to feed the hungry thousands in the growing cities. Drovers brought sheep and cattle over the Scottish border, from the Highlands, the far north of Scotland and the Hebridean islands. Week after week they came, during the summer and autumn season, in continuous processions.

After making their purchases on Wednesday's market day, Morpeth butchers would drive the animals to slaughterhouses behind the buildings on the front street. Other butchers came from nearby towns and walked the animals back along the country lanes. Butchers' shops fronted the main streets, with carcasses hanging in the fresh air. Cutting and sausage-making took place behind. Women customers knew how to cook the meat, and the poorer women could buy offal, or a cheap cut to make a nourishing stew.

This is the story of the drovers, the men who brought their animals along the roads to Morpeth's market, and what happened when they arrived. The roads to the market passed through some of the finest scenery in the country. Some of the journeys were months long, others took weeks or days. It had happened as long as Morpeth had been a town, over many centuries. It still happens, though in a very different way now.

1603 is an important date in this story. In that year, James VI of Scotland travelled to England to become James I of England as well, in what is known as the Union of the Crowns. Trade opened up between the two countries, and Scottish cattle began to be moved south in far greater numbers than before. Many of them came through Morpeth.

In 1686, there is evidence that this traffic caused a furore. The local landowners were outraged because the influx of Scottish cattle lowered the prices they could get for their own animals. Gathering their forces together, they persuaded the jurors at the quarter sessions to present a petition to Parliament.

This is the wording of the petition, which can be seen in Northumberland Archives in a bound volume 1½" thick, 9" wide and 14ins long. It was presented at the Morpeth Quarter Sessions on the 13th of January 1686.[2]

---

[1] J Bailey and B Culley, p 173
[2] Northumberland General Quarter Sessions of the Peace, p 263

"Wee being likewise too much Sensible of the great Prejudice our County Suffers by the Multitudes of Scotch Cattell and Sheep which weekely cloy our Marketts occasioning both these that are bred and fedd within our County to be Sold at Such low Rates that these whose Rents depends upon Grassing will certainly in a Short be Considerably dampnified if not altogether Ruined thereby which greeviance we Suppose to be occasioned by the Expiration of an Act which did formerly prohibitt them att certaine Seasons from comeing into England wee conceive it therefore requisitt and request your worshipps that our Representatives for the County be desired to use their utmost endeavours att the next Session of Parliament for the Compassing of the Renuall of the aforesaid Act."

The landowners much resented that the Scottish animals did "weekely cloy our Marketts". In order to pay their rents, they relied on the sale of their "Grassing", or grazing, cattle. They would be much "dampnified", or injured, if the trade wasn't stopped.

The Justices of the Peace acted as decision-makers at the quarterly sessions. The jurors were asking the JPs, "your worshipps", to request the help of the "Representatives for the County".

They want the Representatives, who were the local members of Parliament, to speak out in the next parliamentary session for the "Renuall", or renewal, of an Act which prohibited the coming of animals at certain seasons to the market.

This is one of the few direct early references to the passing of animals through Morpeth, an early instance of animals coming from Scotland. The act referred to was called "Act Limiting the Times of Importation of Cattle from Scotland".

The Jurors contained names of families still known in our locality.

William Cresswell	George Lawson
Ralph Anderson	Thomas Lawson
John Lawson	Ralph Watson
Mark Aynsley	Martine Baird
Richard Goftin	Rowland Archer
William Reed	Edward Kirton
William Bullocke	Robert Donkin
Robert Bulman	George Potts
William Archbold	

The petition does not appear to have been successful. The Act had passed through its three readings in the House of Commons in 1681, and two in the House of Lords. It was not passed, as this was the period when Charles II was battling with Parliament, and he called no more Parliaments until 1685.[3] The significance to us of this extract from the Quarter Sessions is that it is a rare mention of Highlanders and their cattle in Morpeth's market.

There had always been cattle and sheep sales in Morpeth, ever since the first charter for the market in 1199 under Roger de Merlay II, in the time of King John.

But after 1603, and again at the Union of Parliaments in 1707, the pace of the droving industry between the two countries greatly accelerated. It changed in various ways over the decades, peaking in Morpeth in the first quarter of the nineteenth century.

On Tuesday afternoons over the centuries, as the droves of animals arrived, people in Morpeth would be preparing for the market. In the inns and public houses, the women would be rolling out the pastry for pies, while the steamed meat for the fillings was cooling on the

---

[3] House of Commons and House of Lords Journals
http://british-history.ac.uk/period.aspx?period=7&gid=44). Research by Margaret Madison

2

windowsills. The busy butchers down in the alleys behind their shops would be sharpening their knives and sweeping out their slaughterhouses. The vats in the brewhouses were filled with the bubbling ale. The children as usual were getting under everyone's feet, the babies squalling for attention, and the dogs scavenging among the scraps in hidden corners of the crowded yards. The next day, Wednesday, was market day. It always had been, and it seemed it always would be.

If we could look down on the scene from a bird's eye view, we would see a pattern of lanes, lined with green hedges and trees, leading in to the hub of this Northumbrian town. The lanes come in from every direction. Beside the winding river Wansbeck, flat horseshoe-shaped grassy haughs lie tucked in its curves. Along the lanes, making their slow progress towards the town, are parades of animals, processions of mooings and bellowings, bleatings and baaings, moving towards the centre from every direction but particularly from the north. Behind them, with their sticks and their dogs, the drovers are moving the animals forward.

Morpeth is unusual in that it has a rare surviving personal account from a nineteenth century drover. George Robson drove cattle and sheep to Morpeth regularly between roughly 1790 and 1830. He was interviewed by the correspondent of an unknown publication in about 1850. The undated article mentions the market at Newcastle in 1843 and that George Robson left Morpeth in 1835. At the time of the interview, he was 80 years old, meaning that he was born about 1770. He was interviewed in London where he was running a hotel in Argyle Square, near Kings Cross station. The article is called *The Old Cattle Market at Morpeth: An Old Northumbrian's Recollections*, and it can be seen in Northumberland Archives at Woodhorn.

His interviewer tells us that he was six feet tall, and as straight as any man of thirty; he and his father "had perhaps more to do with that market than any man living".

George Robson recounted that the fat stock market (as distinct from markets for cattle which needed further fattening) had begun in the later 1700s, when the animals were mainly grass fed. As agricultural improvements increased, particularly with turnip husbandry which allowed animals to be fed throughout the winter, there was a large increase in the breeding of sheep and cattle, and the growth of weekly fat markets all over the kingdom. George Robson:

> On Morpeth market day, the sheep were shown in pens in the long, inconvenient yards of the taverns on both sides of the long straggling street, 6 pence per score or pen being charged for sheep. The cattle all stood on each side of the street from the end of the old bridge to the upper end of the square where the old Market House stood. The market was generally over by noon, and I have seen it all over at eight o'clock in the morning in a sharp market.

This was such an important market, he said, that buyers came from the south of Northumberland and the county of Durham, and would arrive at Morpeth on Tuesday afternoon, special coaches being run from Sunderland, Houghton-le-Spring, Tynemouth and Newcastle. In the three spring months, when the winter fed cattle came to market, buyers came from as far away as Leeds and Wakefield.

These are different cattle from the "Scotch Cattell" of the 1686 petition, which would have been smaller black Highland cattle, known as *kyloes*. By the time that George Robson is describing, they are "the primest shorthorn breed, and the sheep principally Leicesters, or hybrid Leicester and Cheviots". George Robson:

> Morpeth was a thriving little town during the time of its cattle market. The innkeepers must have been a very convivial fraternity, as most of the market inns were kept by widows. The first time that I was at Morpeth, about seventy years ago, a very small boy, our hostelry was the Black Bull Inn, kept at the time by a widow named Mrs Stephenson.

George Robson was "a very small boy" probably in the 1780s or 1790s. Inn-keeping must have been a suitable way for widows to be self-supporting. Pigot's Directory of 1822 shows a list of 33 inns, taverns and public houses in Morpeth, and the Black Bull is still in the management of the Stephenson family.

Kings Arms Inn, Bridge St	Elizabeth Whitfield
New Phoenix Inn, Bridge St	Jane Peacock
Old Phoenix Inn and excise, Bridge St	Wm Hogg
Queen's Head Inn and Posting House, Bridge St	Mary Sunderland
Bay Nag's Head, Newgate St	Thos Lackenby
Black and the Grey, Newgate St	Elizabeth Bean
Black Bull, Bridge St	A Stephenson
Black Swan, King St	Adam Hall
Brown Cow, Newgate St	B Watson
Bull's Head, Bridge End	Jno Thompson
Coach and Horses, Market Place	John Riddell
Corporation Inn, Bridge St	Henry Smith
George and Dragon Inn, Bridge St	John Humphrey
Granby Inn, Birdge St	Michael Pattison
Grey Bull, Market Place	Wm Walker
Greyhound, Silver St	Ann Flint
Grey Nag's Head, Newgate St	Sarah Womack
Hope and Anchor, Bridge St	Elizabeth Sadler
Howard's Arms, Bridge St	William Heron
King Crispin, Newgate St	Geo Beaumont
King's Head, Bridge St	John Hedley
Lord Hood, Newgate St	Geo Hood
Old Hope and Anchor, Bridge St	Joseph McLellan
Old Queen's Head, Oldgate	Geo Hedley
Pack Horse, Newgate St	Rt Hudson
Scotch Arms, Market Place	Jno Howe
Seven Stars, Bullers Green	John Dees
Shoulder of Mutton, Newgate St	Mary Hardinge
Spread Eagle, Bridge End	Sarah Nevins
Turk's Head, Bridge St	Frances Thompson
Whalebone Inn, Bridge St	Jane Whitham
Wheat Sheaf, Market Place	Wm Purvis
White Swan, Newgate St	Henry Esther

When George Robson and drovers like him arrived in Morpeth, they would first place the animals safely in fields to be rested, fed and watered. Finding suitable overnight stances for vast numbers of animals was part of the market arrangements. The innkeepers were known to rent out fields in and around Morpeth. The Black Bull on Bridge Street, where George Robson stayed, had its own fields for stock on the land behind where the library is now.[4] These fields adjoin the river Wansbeck, where many animals could go down to drink at the same time. Once the animals were settled, the drovers would attend to their own needs and those of their dogs. Janet Brown has further details in her booklet *Morpeth's Market:*

> The local publicans also owned or rented fields in and around Morpeth for use as holding paddocks. As well as putting up the drovers on a 'donkey's breakfast' (palliasse) for the night, and providing them and the farmers and butchers with their own breakfasts, and dinners on market day, ... the pens and the right to set them up on the road were largely owned by the innkeepers.[5]

Wednesday was market day. We can imagine the noise, the bustle, the lowing and bleating of animals, the shouting of the men, and the children running hither and thither through the mucky streets. Writers throughout the 19th century tell us what it was like at that time:

---

[4] Alec Tweddle, p 19
[5] Janet Brown, p 18

Morpeth is a kind of cattle depot, in its fairs for the district with its great, greasy, glazed-hatted cattle dealers. As we rolled rapidly through the town we lost sight of the cattle dealers and came into the midst of a number of fine gingerbread stalls, stalls for the sale of tea trays, toys, knives, saddles, cheese and china. The pretty maidens in their holiday ribbons were chattering and cheapening, and all seemed lively and happy.
An unnamed traveller reporting in Newcastle Magazine, 1822, Morpeth's Market, p 21

The Market Place is conveniently situated near the centre of the town, but is not sufficiently capacious for the numerous droves of cattle, flocks of sheep, swine, etc. which are here exposed for sale. The sheep pens partly front the shops, leaving a narrow passage to the doors, and are partly set up in narrow lanes and courts adjoining the market place.
Parson and White's directory, 1827, p 450

The privilege of holding a weekly market here on Wednesdays was first granted to Roger de Merlay the Second by King John, in 1190. The great *cattle market* holden here grew … from very small beginnings to its present consequence. At present, every horned beast coming in to this market for sale, pays 1d; every score of sheep, 4d; every pig and calf, ½d. The weekly sale of oxen here has now for many years been upwards of 200, and of sheep and lambs 2,500, which are chiefly reared and fed in Northumberland and Scotland, and consumed within the limits of the trade and ports of the Tyne and Wear. Part of them go as far as Leeds and Manchester; and when the demand for fat cattle is brisk in the south, considerable quantities are purchased here for the London market.
John Hodgson, History of Morpeth, 1832, p77

Cattle and sheep were brought into the town from Scotland, and from Cumberland. The Greys, Culley, Adam Atkinson, Johnson and Fenwick, large farmers of Northumberland, brought their own stock to market, most of them arriving on Tuesday night, as did the principal butchers … reaching the town almost as soon as it was light in summer, and in winter before the sun rose. Upon a sale being agreed, the purchaser took a shilling from his pocket, which he spit upon and offered to the seller, who, if he accepted the bid, took the shilling, or *arles,* and the bargain was binding. A man stood at the north end of Morpeth bridge to levy the tolls for the lord of the manor, viz. for every head of cattle 1d, for a score of sheep 4d, and for a pig or calf ½d.
William Woodman, from 1835, Morpeth's Market, p 16.

Herds of shaggy cattle and droves of sheep are huddled in the streets, horses are trotted hither and thither to show off their paces; dogs are heard barking and yelping furiously; old cattle drovers – unique specimens of humanity – shuffle before our eyes like the sole survivors of a bygone generation. Now and again, you would see a farmer's daughter, whose carriage and appearance would grace Bond Street or Regent Street, carrying a large basket of eggs or butter, or at other times helping her father to drive some of their four-legged purchases back to their farm.
Edmund Bogg, A Thousand Miles of Wandering in the Border Country, 1898, p 79

The animals which were not moving beyond Morpeth would be driven to their destinations, down the little alleys and back streets. The 1852 maps of Morpeth produced for the Local Board of Health show five slaughterhouses in the town centre.[6] They were behind Oldgate, roughly where Oldgate Court is now; behind the Market Place, near the yard of the Wheatsheaf Inn where the coffee shop is now; to the north of Bridge Street, behind the Hope and Anchor Inn, which was between Corporation Yard and the Black Bull Inn; and on Dogger Bank.

---

[6] Plan of the Town and Part of the Borough of Morpeth, 1852

Photo: Morpeth market place in the early twentieth century. Keith Creighton collection

Pigot's 1822 directory lists twenty five butchers, three skinners, three tanners, two curriers and leather cutters, four saddlers, two glovers, two tallow chandlers, and ten boot and shoe makers. For Morpeth, producing meat and associated products was fundamental.

An indication of the increase in the number of animals sold in Morpeth's market over the years can be found in various publications.

	cattle	sheep	
1686	20,000 in one year	190,000 in one year	The number for which tolls were paid to cross Morpeth bridge, Cowper, p 31
1761	40 weekly	600 weekly	*Morpeth: its Cattle Market and its Inns,*
1794	80 weekly	1600 weekly	Bailey & Culley, p 174
1811	100 weekly	2000 weekly	*Morpeth: its Cattle Market and its Inns,*
1827	200 weekly	2500 weekly	Parson & White directory p 450
1832	200 weekly	2500 weekly	John Hodgson p 77
1835	20595 annually	149,287 lambs sheep and pigs annually	Edmund Bowman, quoted in *Morpeth's Market*, p 30
1841	20893 annually		George Strachan p 7

There don't appear to be any contemporary descriptions of the passing of large droves of cattle and sheep south along the Great North Road through Morpeth, but Edmund Bogg wrote about what he saw further south in Boroughbridge and Wetherby.[7] At these places, droves would have accumulated from other cross-Pennine and north/south routes. So although it is not possible to claim that such numbers passed through Morpeth, his writing nevertheless gives a flavour of what it must have been like at times:

> Immense droves of cattle - half wild - and sheep in charge of drovers, were generally on the move from north to south ... Two thousand cattle passed through Boroughbridge daily when the droves were on the move ... Many a time from sunrise to sunset have the streets of Wetherby never for a moment been free from cattle. Drove after drove passed through the town, and individual herds have been known to pack the road for fully half-a-mile of its length.

---

[7] Edmund Bogg, quoted by William Thompson, p 179

The vast numbers of animals crossing from Scotland over the Borders to England were described by William Thomson in his article, *Cattle Droving between Scotland and England.*[8] Although the figures refer mainly to the west coast droving routes, they give an idea of the size of the traffic.

1533	10,336	10,336 cattle, 12,492 sheep, 1,296 horses and 200 goats brought back in one raid over the Border from Scotland
1662	318,574	318,574 cattle passed through Carlisle in that year at a toll of 8 pence her head. The number excludes those which passed through illegally
1663 - 1699	15,000	15,000 cattle crossed the Scottish frontier annually between these dates
1684	20,000	at least 20,000 cattle passed over the Nith Bridge at Dumfries, earning £700 in tolls
1784 – 1789	10,700	average annually imported from Ireland at Port Patrick

After the arrival of the main north south railway line to Morpeth, in 1847, its market suffered a rapid decline. But until that time, there was no way to bring the animals other than on foot. The drovers brought them along; the kilt-swinging, bold, adventurous and competent drovers; who knew their way over the hills and along the lanes; who travelled sometimes hundreds of miles, driving enormous herds and flocks; and who arrived on the appointed day without fail.

---

[8] William Thompson, pp 174 - 176

Highland drovers coming down Newgate Street, 1686

The Highland drovers, and those like George Robson and the men he travelled with on the way to Morpeth, are the heroes of this story. Living as we do in these comfortable times, it is hard to realise how tough they were, how intelligent, enduring and adventurous, and yet in many cases how poor. The Highlanders who brought the "Multitudes of Scotch Cattell and Sheep which weekely cloy our Marketts" take us back to the days when our two nations were only just beginning to feel at ease with each other. Even after the crushing of the 1715 and 1745 Jacobite rebellions, journeying between Scotland and England was still so dangerous that drovers were exempted from the Disarming Acts of 1716 and 1748, and were issued licences permitting them to carry gun, sword or pistol.[9]

We can learn something about what it was like to be a drover, and to understand these men who drove their animals through the streets of Morpeth, from writers of the time.

Edmund Burt was an agent for General Wade, writing in the mid 1720s. His work, *Letters Concerning Scotland*, tells us about the poverty of the villages in the Highlands, from where many of the drovers came:[10]

> A Highland town is composed of a few huts for dwellings, with barns and stables ... all irregularly placed, some one way, some another, and at any distance look like so many heaps of dirt.
>
> Spring is a bad season for them; for then their provision of oatmeal begins to fail, and for a supply they bleed their cattle, and boil the blood into cakes, which together with a little milk and a short allowance of oatmeal, is their food.
>
> This immoderate bleeding reduces the cattle to so low a plight, that in a morning they cannot rise from the ground, and several of the inhabitants join together to help up each other's cows.
>
> In summer, the people remove to the hills, and dwell in much worse huts than those they leave below: these are near the spots of grazing, and are called *shealings*. Here they make their butter and cheese.
>
> About the latter end of August or the beginning of September the cattle are brought into good order by their summer feed, and the beef is extremely sweet and succulent; which I suppose is owing, in good part, to their being reduced to such poverty in the spring, and made up again with new flesh.
>
> Now the drovers collect their herds, and drive them to fairs and markets on the borders of the Lowlands, and sometimes to the North of England; and in their passage they pay a certain tribute, proportionable to the number of cattle, to the owner of the territory they pass through.

Burt also describes the clothing of those who travel on foot:

> The common habit of the ordinary Highlanders is far from being acceptable to the eye ... the plaid "is set in folds and girt round the waist to make a short petticoat that reaches half way down the thigh, and the rest is brought over the shoulders and then fastened before, below the neck, often with a fork, and sometimes with a bodkin or sharpened piece of stick ... In this way of wearing the plaid, they have sometimes nothing else to cover them, and are often barefoot; but some I have seen shod with a kind of pumps made out of a raw cowhide with the hair turned outward, which being ill made, the wearer's feet looked something like those of a rough-footed hen or pigeon: these are called *quarrants,* and are not only offensive to the sight but intolerable to the smell of those who are near them.
>
> The stocking rises no higher than the thick of the calf, and from the middle of the thigh to the middle of the leg is a naked space, which being exposed to all weathers, becomes tanned and

---

[9] A R B Haldane, p 25
[10] Edward Burt, pp 99 - 101 and 114 - 117

freckled; and the joint being mostly infected with the country distemper, the whole is very disagreeable to the eye.

This dress is called the *quelt;* and for the most part they wear the petticoat so very short, that in a windy day, going up a hill, or stooping, the indecency of it is plainly discovered.

The plaid serves the ordinary people for a cloak by day and bedding at night: by the latter it imbibes so much perspiration, that no one day can free it from the filthy smell; and even some of better than ordinary appearance, when the plaid falls from the shoulder, or otherwise requires to be re-adjusted, while you are talking with them, toss it over again, which conveys the offence in whiffs that are intolerable: of this they seem not to be sensible, for it is often done only to give themselves airs.

It renders them ready at a moment's warning to join in any rebellion, as they carry continually their tents about them. On the other hand it is alleged, the dress is most convenient to those who, with no ill design, are obliged to travel from one part to another upon their lawful occasions, viz. That they would not be so free to skip over the rocks and bogs with breeches, as they are in the short petticoat"... That even if they should be so fortunate as to reach some hospitable hut, they must lie upon the ground uncovered, there being nothing to be spared from the family for that purpose.

Sir Walter Scott knew the droving trade at first hand, and wrote about it in his short story of 1827, *The Two Drovers*:[11]

Many large droves were about to set off for England, under the protection of their owners, or of the topsmen whom they employed in the tedious, laborious, and responsible office of driving the cattle for many hundreds of miles, from the market where they had been purchased to the fields or farm-yards where they were to be fattened for the shambles.

The Highlanders are masters of this difficult trade of driving which seems to suit them as well as the trade of war. It affords exercise for all their habits of patient endurance and active exertion. They are required to know perfectly the drove roads which lie over the wildest tracts of country, and to avoid as much as possible the highways, which distress the feet of the bullocks, and the turnpikes, which annoy the spirit of the drover; whereas on the broad green or grey track, which leads across the pathless moor, the herd not only move at ease and without taxation, but if they mind their business, may pick up a mouthful of food by the way."

At night, the drovers usually sleep along with their cattle, let the weather be what it will; and many of these hardy men do not once rest under a roof during a journey on foot from Lochaber to Lincolnshire.

They are paid very highly, for the trust reposed is of the last importance, as it depends on their prudence, vigilance, and honesty, whether the cattle reach the final market in good order, and afford a profit to the grazier.

But as they maintain themselves at their own expense, they are especially economical in that particular. A Highland drover was victualled for his long and toilsome journey with a few handfuls of oatmeal and two or three onions, renewed from time to time, and a ram's horn filled with whisky, which he used regularly, but sparingly, every night and morning.

Robin Oig McCombich is one of the two drovers in the story. He has already taken several droves south to England. On this particular day, he is setting off again, from his home town of Doune, with the help of some laddies who are his sister's sons. He is taking cattle on behalf of other farmers in the district, and some which he has purchased himself. He hopes that after a few more journeys to England, he might be able to conduct business on his own account:

Though small of stature ... he was as light and alert as one of the deer of his mountains. He had an elasticity of step, which, in the course of a long march, made many a stout fellow envy him; and the manner in which he busked his plaid and adjusted his bonnet, argued a consciousness that so smart a John Highlandman as himself would not pass unnoticed among the Lowland

---

[11] Sir Walter Scott, *The Two Drovers,* pp 124 - 146

10

lasses … The departure of Robin Oig was an incident in the little town, in and near which he had many friends male and female … The bonny lasses made their adieus modestly, and more than one, it was said, would have given her best brooch to be certain that it was upon her that his eye last rested as he turned towards his road.

As he left, the townspeople wished him luck, hoping that he would bring back plenty of English gold. Robin's departure must have typified that of many of the young drovers leaving for the long and dangerous journey.

There must have been some young lasses who would like to have travelled with the herds, and who weren't content to make modest adieus. "Mother, why can't I go?" I can hear one say. "Och Mhaire, only laddies can be drovers," the mother would reply. And the girl, longing to have her own adventures, would stomp off to milk her cow, saying to herself: "It is nae fair!"

There is a sad end to this story, which involves a conflict when Robin Oig kills his English drover friend Harry Wakefield in a duel, and in his turn is led away to the gallows. The route they travelled in this story was down the western side of the country. Nevertheless, in previous droves, they had come through Northumberland. We know this because, at one point in the dispute between the friends, a man challenges Harry, saying: "Sure Harry Wakefield, the nattiest lad at Whitson Tryste, Wooler Fair, Carlisle Sands or Stagshaw Bank, is not going to show the white feather? Ah, this comes of living so long with kilts and bonnets – men forget the use of their daddles." The Whitson Tryste was a fair held at Whitsuntide at Wooler. Stagshaw Bank is just north of Corbridge where fairs were held at Whitsun and Midsummer.[12]

Robin retraces his steps at the point in the story where he wants to get his dirk from another drover in whose safe keeping it had been placed, and whose herd is a few miles behind his own. The story paints a picture of the slowly moving herds:

When Robin Oig left the door of the alehouse, seven or eight English miles at least lay betwixt Morrison and him. The advance of the former was slow, limited by the sluggish pace of his cattle; the last left behind him stubble-field and hedge-row, crag and dark heath, all glittering with frost-rhime in the broad November moonlight, at the rate of six miles an hour. And now the distant lowing of Morrison's cattle is heard; and now they are seen creeping like moles in size and slowness of motion on the broad face of the moor.

Harry's lack of Gaelic and Robin's minimal English reminds us that the two entirely unrelated languages were both spoken in the north of our country at that time. As we know that Highlanders came through Morpeth, it is possible that some dealers in the town would have found it worthwhile to know a few words of Gaelic. There is a report that "in the early part of the 18th century, Mr J. M. Bates, of Aydon White House, bought a Gaelic grammar in order to acquire enough of the language to converse with the Highland Drovers of Stagshaw Bank who could speak hardly any English".[13]

Robert Louis Stevenson is another writer who gives us a glimpse of droving in the early nineteenth century. There were no maps in regular use then, and roads were generally unmarked over wild countryside. Those who needed to travel in the same direction might join the drovers, who acted as their guides. Stevenson's tale is about a young gentleman French soldier called St Ives who escapes from a prison in Edinburgh, and who is helped over the border hills to England by joining two drovers, Sim and Candlish.[14]

In the words of St Ives, Stevenson is rather less flattering than Scott. Sim is a "rough-looking thick-set man", whose first greeting to St Ives is "an inarticulate grumble of sound". He walked with "an ugly roll".

---

[12] Walter Scott, explanatory notes, p 351
[13] K J Bonser, p 134
[14] Robert Louis Stevenson, Chapter 10

They walked together over the hills of the Scottish Borders and Northumberland, as far as Newcastle. A few extracts from the chapter give a flavour of what the journey was like:

> They were dressed in the same coarse homespun, carried similar sticks, were equally begrimed about the nose with snuff, and each wound in an identical plaid of what is called the shepherd's tartan.

> Presently we were ascending the side of the mountain by a rude green track, whose presence I had not hitherto observed. A continual sound of munching, and the crying of a great quantity of moor birds accompanied our progress, which the deliberate pace and perennial appetite of the cattle rendered wearisomely slow. In the midst, my two conductors marched in a contented silence that I could not but admire.

> Sim produced from the corner of his plaid a black bottle, and we all drank and pledged each other. This little ceremony was repeated at becoming intervals, generally after an ascent. Occasionally we shared a mouthful of ewe-milk cheese and an inglorious form of bread, which I understood to be called "shearer's bannock".

> I had the more occasion to remark the extraordinarily desolate nature of that country, through which the drove road continued, hour after hours and even day after day, to wind. A continual succession of insignificant shaggy hills, divided by the course of ten thousand brooks, through which we had to wade, or by the side of which we encamped at night; infinite perspectives of heather, infinite quantities of moorfowl; here and there, by a stream side, small and pretty clumps of willows or the silver birch; here and there, the ruins of ancient and inconsiderable fortresses – made the character of the scene.

> Occasionally, in the distance, we could perceive the smoke of a small town or of an isolated farmhouse or cottage on the moors; more often, a flock of sheep and its attendant shepherd, or a rude field of agriculture perhaps not yet harvested. With these alleviations, we might almost be said to pass through an unbroken desert – sure, one of the most impoverished in Europe.

Eventually, after being set upon by drovers from another herd, the reasons for which are not made clear, and in which St Ives kills one of the attackers, they reached the Great North Road. Disappointingly, Morpeth is not mentioned. St Ives leaves the drovers and prepares to disguise himself as a Scot as he travels further through England:

> At Newcastle, which was the first town I reached, I completed my preparations for the part, before going to the inn, by the purchase of a knapsack and a pair of leathern gaiters. My plaid I continued to wear from sentiment. It was warm, useful to sleep in if I were again benighted, and I had discovered it not unbecoming for a man of gallant carriage.

Another writer, Robert Surtees, included an encounter with a drover in his 1845 book, *Hillingdon Hall*.[15] Mr Jorrocks is a Londoner who has made his fortune, and who has purchased a property in the countryside.

> Mr Jorrocks sauntered on, now across the greensward, now hip-high in waving corn through the field path … now roaming again upon the wilder turf, sprinkled with heather and field flowers. At length he got into one of those now rarely met with passages, a green lane. Scarce a cart-rut broke its even surface, and its verdure was kept close nipped by cattle … It was one of those continuous lines of by-roads frequented chiefly by cattle-drovers … Broader places widening into patches of common towards the hill-tops (over which these roads always pass), furnished cheap pasture for the loitering cattle.

> As luck would have it, just as our Squire got to the narrowest path of this green lane … he encountered a large drove of Scotch kyloes, picking their way as they went. There might be fifty or sixty of them, duns, browns, mottles, reds and blacks, with wildness depicted in the prominent eyes of their broad faces.

> He now got a sight of the drover … He was a tall ungainly-looking man, in a Scotch cap, with the lower part of his face muffled up in a plaid, which, spreading in ample fold across his chest, was

---

[15] Robert Surtees, pp 256 - 259

12

confined by the fringed end under the right arm. A rudely-cast shamrock and thistle decorated the red and grey border of the woollen cap, in which was stuck a splendid eagle's feather. Long, straggling, iron-grey locks escaped from below the cap's close-fitting sides, making the aquiline nose and bright hazel eyes of the wearer more conspicuous.

The drover turned out to be known to Mr Jorrocks. His name was James Pigg. He was wearing a green tartan jacket, a red-stained waistcoat, a pair of baggy, drab breeches, and gaiters decorated with many coloured buttons. He had driven the cattle down from Newcastle, and the pair sat on the drover's plaid, exchanging news, while the cattle picked at the grass.[16]

The drovers who came to Morpeth, or passed through the town on their way south, could have fitted any of those descriptions, over the decades though which they came. They could have been like Burt's poverty stricken Highlanders in the earlier days, those whose arrival caused the depression of prices resulting in the Morpeth landowners' petition in 1686. They could have been like Scott's able, fit young Robin Oig McCombich, or Stevenson's blunt Sim and Candlish. Let us hope they were not like those in the clownish description of James Pigg. Probably the later ones were like the sensible sounding George Robson. Whatever they looked like, it is certain that they needed to be good businessmen and good husbandmen, with an excellent knowledge of the landscapes they were crossing.

Drovers' dogs

Dogs were an essential part of the lives of drovers. A story which turns up here and there has its origin in a footnote in The Drove Roads of Scotland, *p26. In her childhood in the 1840s, a lady had regularly seen collie dogs making their way home unaccompanied. After making enquiries, she was told that these were dogs belonging to drovers who had taken cattle to England. The dogs were turned loose find their own way north. They would follow the route taken on the southward journey, being fed at inns or farms where the drovers had 'stanced', and in the following year when the drovers were again on the way south, they paid for the food given to the dogs. The author A R B Haldane suggests that the dogs may have belonged to drovers who had remained in the south through the autumn for the harvest, when the dogs would not be needed. But this is one of those Chinese whispers stories, and I find it hard to believe that it happened regularly.*

I told the story to Stewart Wallace, a shepherd who works and trains sheepdogs at Prendwick in Northumberland. Like me, he raised a sceptical eyebrow, but he had plenty of praise for good dogs. "The dogs would be trained to go ahead, and when they met other sheep in the way, they would set them away to the hill, and let the drove through. They would never let them get mixed up. Any good dog would be able to do that."

Sandy Mackay, a Scottish shepherd, was talking to writer Matt Mundell about his work, in the early 20th century. "We always had good dogs. They were good road dogs. They were good hill dogs too, but it was a different kind of dog we had in those days. They were the kind which did not need many orders. They would go along the sides of the drove and watch the gates themselves to prevent sheep going through. That was the way to train a dog – on the road with the hoggs." Country Diary, Matt Mundell, p 17

Nancy Moscrop of Harbottle has a story about Yid, a Scottish drover, at Uswayford farm where she lived at the time. "Yid was standing by the gate, with his dog, shedding the sheep. Shedding means sorting them. The dog only let the Blackface sheep through, and not the Cheviots. He was that clever."

Here is the young St Ives on the dogs of drovers Sim and Candlish.

"Beautiful, indefatigable beings! As I saw them at the end of a long day's journey, frisking, barking, bounding, striking attitudes, slanting a bushy tail, manifestly playing to the spectator's eye, manifestly rejoicing in their grace and beauty … My sympathy was unreturned; in their eyes I was a creature light as air; and they would scarce spare me the time for a perfunctory caress or perhaps a hasty lap of the wet tongue, ere they were back again in sedulous attendance on those dingy deities, their masters – and their masters as like as not, damning their stupidity."

---

[16] Robert Surtees, pp 256 - 259

Mrs Wardle giving the drovers their breakfast at the inn on Rimside Moor, 1820

A ramshorn of whisky and a bag of crispy oatmeal biscuits; a green road stretching south over the hills; herds of shaggy-haired black cattle nibbling at the wayside grasses; white clouds sailing along in the breeze; the scent of wild flowers in the air.   The drovers of old are coming to Morpeth town.

Such imaginings are the stuff of dreams. Living in this town, at a focus of routes which drovers used in the past as they brought their animals to market, we can think ourselves into almost-forgotten days; and follow their footsteps.

Almost every road in the countryside before the age of motor traffic could be said to have been a drove road. Wherever there are farms, animals have to be moved. All the roads to market towns would have had cattle, sheep and other animals moving along them at various times, as well as horses used for every form of transport. We are especially fortunate to have a detailed description from George Robson about one particular route which he followed to Morpeth.

The long distance drovers like the Highlanders and George Robson were husbandmen. The daily needs of the animals determined how the drovers proceeded. I learned much of what follows from the most readable of books on this subject, *The Drove Roads of Scotland* by Scottish writer A R B Haldane.[17]

The largest droves, heading for the most important fairs in both Scotland and England could number thousands, and stretched for several miles. There would be one man for every fifty or sixty animals, with a couple of lads and a few dogs.

The drovers needed to know the route in great detail. Every single day's journey, every night's stop, had to be calculated. Wet weather could make rivers dangerous or impassible, and dry weather reduce the amount of grass on the way, or the availability of suitable watering places:

> The beasts must not be hurried, especially during the first days of the march, and the usual day's journey was ten to twelve miles. At midday the drovers halted to allow the cattle to graze, and when evening came they stopped in some suitable spot where the beasts could rest, graze and drink, while the men passed the night wrapped in their plaids in such shelter as the place afforded, but always on the watch to guard the drove or to do such herding as the tired beasts needed … When morning came the beasts were quietly roused and collected again for the road, for cattle startled and hurried after a night's rest were liable to scatter and stampede.[18]

The animals crossed the open moors and hills, in their hundreds and thousands over the years. They followed traditional routes, and the mere fact of their passing had an effect on the surfaces. Their hooves would cut into the land, creating hollowed pathways. When the land was wet, the cattle created muddy ruts which they would avoid by diverting sideways, thus creating parallel tracks, just as hikers do now on popular country paths. These tracks have become known as hollow ways, or holloways. They often spread upward from a ford over a stream, or from a "pinch point" on the hillside where the shape of the land had forced the animals to funnel together.

Holloways, fords, watering points for animals, inns and public houses providing shelter and refreshment for the drovers all give clues about the routes the drovers took, and we can see evidence of them along the roads to Morpeth.

The route described by George Robson tells about evening stops along the turnpike road between Coldstream and Morpeth.[19] However he does not specifically say that they followed the turnpike and paid the tolls at the gates. Writing about this road, Ian Roberts wrote: "It is

---

[17] A R B Haldane pp 29 - 44
[18] A R B Haldane pp 35 - 38
[19] George Robson, *The Old Cattle Market at Morpeth*

possible that, following turnpiking of the road in the mid-eighteenth century, drovers avoided sections of the road by taking smaller parallel tracks to the west." "A minor road running between farms parallel with the west side of the A697 may also have been used by drovers as far as Powburn, Glanton and Whittingham."[20]

Intrigued by this possibility, in the summer of 2011 my friend Mary and I decided to follow the ways the drovers could practically have used, avoiding the toll gates. We loaded up our bicycles with the essential supplies, the whisky and oatmeal, tents and camping gear. We chose minor roads and bridle paths, to the west of the A697. As we went, we imagined ourselves into the landscape which the drovers would have seen.

Most of the route can be cycled or walked along back roads and bridle ways. We did it as a linear route, taking the train and bus to Berwick and Coldstream, and then heading for Morpeth. Equally, it could be done in parts after driving to a suitable spot. If you are an armchair traveller, you can just sit back and accompany Mary and me, as we follow this exhilarating droving road through Northumberland.

The distance is about fifty miles, and it took George Robson with his companion drovers and their animals five days. In his newspaper interview, he described the route they took each day, timing the journey so that they would arrive in Morpeth on Tuesday, the day before the Wednesday market. As far as we can tell, he made this journey frequently in the later years of the eighteenth century, and the first decades of the nineteenth century. The selections which follow in bold are his words.

Friday   Crossing the Tweed at Coldstream
"Of course the stock were all driven by road, being lifted from Roxburgh and Berwickshire on the Fridays, crossing the Tweed at Kelso and Coldstream, and stopping generally at some farm place the first night."

As George Robson and his fellow drovers moved the cattle through the main street of Coldstream, it would occasion some interest, women turning their heads aside from the smell, and flicking their skirts away from the dust thrown up by the hooves of the animals; children staring. But generally not a lot of attention would be paid to the procession. It happened all the time in those days.

The drovers would guide their brown and white shorthorned cattle towards the bridge crossing the River Tweed into England. They were heading for Morpeth, where the animals must arrive on the Tuesday following, in time for the market on Wednesday. The cattle were docile, used to being driven, and the men moved them forward with care, cautiously, so as not to alarm them.

On the approach to the bridge, the drovers would glance at the Cheviot foothills on the southern horizon. They would notice the horseshoe-shaped haugh on the other side of the River Tweed, a flat loop in the course of the river. At one time there was a ford there, and over the river a possible lairage, or enclosure, for cattle or sheep (NT 855385).[21] Before the building of the bridge in 1766, the drovers would have had to use the fords.

The older drovers would surely remember stories about these river crossings. The Jacobite uprising of 1745 will still have been a topic of conversation among them. The bridge and beginnings of improved roads were partly an attempt by the government to allow armies to move more freely into Scotland, following the rebellion.

---

[20] Ian Roberts, p 115
[21] Roy's Military Map, 1755

The drovers would pass a bonny little tollhouse at the entrance to the bridge. Maybe this time, or on another occasion, they would encounter an eloping couple, making a hasty marriage there.

Coldstream bridge toll house. From Edmund Bogg, 1898

Coldstream marriage

"Married at Coldstream by Especial Licence, W. Ephraim Dixon, Wine Merchant, Morpeth, to Elizabeth Coull, daughter of Robert Coull Esq. Thornton, my niece, on or about 21 September and was Married over again at Morpeth Church on Monday the 29th Sept. She Eliz was paying a visit at Mr Reeds, Birness near Jedburgh & Mr Dixon taken the opportunity of going in a Post Chase and taken her away to Coldstream, unknown to either <u>Father</u> or <u>Mother</u> makes it very disagreeable to pairent however such things has been done before & likewise may be done again."

From The Diaries of William Brewis of Mitford, 1834, *p 19*

Once over the bridge, the drovers headed for "some farm place", on the way to Cornhill on the southern side of the Tweed. They would have had enough travelling for one day, having gathered the cattle up from a variety of farms in Roxburghshire and Berwickshire, and then getting over the border into England.

Saturday   Cornhill to Bendor
"The next night's stopping place was Bendor, Saturday night, at a small inn north of Wooler, 33 miles from Morpeth, with fields attached for the accommodation of stock."

Cornhill is an important village, on the junction of the Berwick to Kelso and the Coldstream to Morpeth roads. The early 19th century Collingwood Arms hotel is an old coaching inn, as the sign "Post House" over the doorway reminds us.

After 1806, the drovers had the choice at Cornhill of going along the turnpikes to Bendor and paying the tolls, or using alternative open routes which we are going to follow, to the west.

The dismantled railway embankments that we pass by on the way to East Learmouth are like a phantom of the past. Steam travel would not have entered the wildest imagination of the early drovers, yet since their time the railways have come, had their day, and gone again. These railway tracks led west/east between Kelso and Berwick, and south to Mindrum.

The scent of wayside flowers is in the air, golden ladies' bedstraw, creamy meadowsweet, and scrambling purple vetches. Yellowhammers are calling out their little-bit-of-bread-and-no-cheese song. The drovers' cattle would move easily between the hedgerows, ambling along, taking the steep places in their stride, munching on bites of flowers and grass on the banks. Mary and I greet a woman coming down the hill on horseback. We share a comment on the pleasant weather of the day,

We have to push our bikes up some hills. The minor roads often have steeper gradients, and our folding bikes have only a few gears. Drovers had a different attitude to gradients.

Haldane describes a route in Argyll where the drovers took the shortest line up and over the mountains and lochs.

> It is well to bear in mind the difference between the outlook of a drover of the times, and that of a traveller of today. To a drover, the successive barriers of hills, sea and inland lochs presented few obstacles, for the hills offered firm going, good grazing and resting-places for beasts at night.[22]

Between the turnpike road and our minor road is the site of the 1513 Battle of Flodden, the place names reminding us of it. The big stone cross on the battle site is modern.

The Battle of Flodden

On 9 September 1513 an English army led by Thomas Howard, Earl of Surrey, confronted a Scottish army under King James IV. The day was a military disaster for Scotland. It was reported that 10,000 Scots were killed in the battle, including the king and a large number of the Scottish nobility. The agony of that dreadful defeat is still remembered in the ancient Common Ridings of Selkirk and Hawick, and also in the modern Coldstream Civic Week.

It is likely that the drovers of George Robson's time would have some knowledge of the battle. In the 1790s, the Common Riding Song was composed for Hawick by Arthur Balburnie, including the words:

> *At Flodden Field our fathers fought it*
> *And honour gain'd*
> *though dear they bought it.*

Extracted from Scotland's Common Ridings, *Kenneth R Bogle, pp 77 - 78*

At last, we reach the crest of the hill beyond East Moneylaws. The Cheviot range appears strong and bold in front of us, but our route will circle the hills to the east, the way Scottish drovers could choose if they wanted to avoid the Cheviots.

---
[22] A R B Haldane, p87

Mary and I descend easily downhill to Milfield. It is another four miles to the evening stance at Bendor.

Now we are in the low and fertile farmlands, this time of the Till valley. Cycling is easy. We cross to the other side of the A697 at Milfield. At Maelmin, (NT 942337) the prehistoric settlement site has been reconstructed to show the successive phases of history along this valley, but there was nothing to be seen there when the drovers passed by. We cycle along shaded lanes by Ewart Park, and the gliding club. There are big stone gateposts, the fields in the flat floodplain full of grazing animals. Ewart Park played a role in twentieth century shepherding in the Cheviot area, providing temporary grazing for hill flocks.

Droving to Ewart Parks

"The drove road and right of way to Ewart Parks from places on the east side of the river Till ran right through the fields that lay beyond the river. Ewart Grass Parks had been in existence for many, many years before we went to Glendale, and are still being let at the present day ... Most of the cattle were accompanied by men on horseback, which was a better way of controlling a herd, especially during the difficult drive through fields where cattle were grazing.

"Grass parks have always played a part in the economy of Borders stock farming. They were let annually for grazing either by public roup or private bargain, for the period March to December. Farmers rented grass parks to gain additional grazing in summer and autumn, thus enabling them to keep more stock. In the case of the hill farms, the taking of grass parks was principally to get better grazing for the ewes with twin lambs, for which the ordinary hill ground was not adequate. A resident shepherd was provided to tend the stock at the parks, and this was a job often given to an elderly man, who would undertake estate work when the parks were empty."

Andrew Purves, 1940s, p 201 and 191 - 192

Cyclists like us, or people out for a quiet drive and a picnic, can enjoy this flat flood plain where the Rivers Till and Glen come together. This is Glendale. New maps show the national cycling route 68 going south from Norham-on-Tweed to Wooler, passing Ford, along these back roads. Undoubtedly we are in the tracks used by drovers and local people moving animals, as Andrew Purves has shown. One of the quiet lanes leads to the former Black Bull inn at Bendor, at the end of George Robson's Saturday drove.

In the earlier days of George Robson's droving life, the Glendale area had become renowned for farming improvements. Until these times, drovers had few hedges and fences to impede them. The 1805 report by the agriculturalists J Bailey and G Culley describes the enclosures, which would have affected droving. "The parts of this country capable of cultivation, are in general well enclosed by live hedges." Referring to the vales of Breamish, Till and Glen, they state that "this, in 1804, is nearly accomplished, there being now very few unenclosed farms."[23]

George Robson and his drover companions stayed at the Black Bull inn at Bendor for the night. The animals needed watering, and it is likely that they used the River Glen nearby. The toll gate here could be negotiated in the morning, and they could use the services of the smithy. In *Drove Roads of Northumberland*, Ian Roberts' photo is labelled "The Black Bull, former drovers' inn at Bendor", and he mentions "the roof space of which contained cubicled divisions for individual drovers on their first night out of Cornhill".[24]

---

[23] J Bailey and G Culley, p 60
[24] Ian Roberts, p 115

Black Bess and the Black Bull at Bendor

Patsy and Bunce Morton lived at the former Black Bull at Bendor most of their married lives. They recently moved into a nearby cottage. Bunce said: "My granddad moved to the house that used to be the Black Bull in 1875. The floors were earthen. I came here when I was two years old, in 1927. When I was a boy, you just stepped right out of the house onto the road. When you went in the front door, you went straight up two staircases to the attic. It had a wooden floor in my day, and you looked straight up to the tiled roof and the rafters."

The Black Bull had fields for the drovers' animals, one on the Wooler side, and two behind the inn. These were the fields belonging to the house when Bunce lived there.

Patsy Morton's granddad was a rabbit catcher. "He used to call in to the Black Bull for a pint, with his rabbits tied in pairs. It would be in the 1890s or early 1900s." She remembers hearing that the drovers would use land at nearby High Humbledon. "It was free land, common land."

Both Patsy and Bunce remember the toll cottage and Black Bess who lived there, although the gate had gone by their time.

Sybil Straughan, who was born in 1925, lived with her parents in the station master's house at nearby Akeld. She also remembers the toll cottage, and Black Bess with her many children. "The toll house was a simple country cottage. I would walk along the road with the other children on the way to school in Wooler. The children in the house were never ready, and we used to try to peep in to see what it was like inside, while their mother was preparing something for them to eat for their dinner."

Kathy Morton is Bunce and Patsy's sister-in-law. Her father used to drop in to the Black Bull for a pint in the early twentieth century. He used to tell her about the famous Bendor monkey, who would pick up coins from the bar. Some men decided that they would pay the monkey back, and they heated up the coins in the fire so that it burnt its finger. It never touched the coins again. "Here also was a blacksmith's shop, where the cattle could be shod on their long journeys south to the market," according to an undated newspaper article in the ownership of the Mortons.

Some time in the early twentieth century, the Black Bull ceased to be an inn. During the 1950s, the toll cottage was taken down. Now there is simply an empty lay-by in its place, where drivers can park their car, and imagine the scenes of long ago.

The Black Bull Inn, from an undated painting donated by Bunce and Patsy Morton.

20

This is the first night for Mary and me, following the path of the drovers. We are establishing our camp for the night behind a handy wall on a hillside, when a big black cloud approaches from the south west. We've assembled the tents, got out the whisky bottle, and Mary is lighting the stove for the oatmeal, when the rain arrives. It comes down in torrents, in sheets. We can't imagine how drovers had to sleep outside in such conditions. For us grandmother drover-followers of the twenty-first century, there is no question of enduring it. We cycle into Wooler and drip all over the hallway of a cosy bed-and-breakfast. It reminds us that whatever the weather, the drovers would have to keep to their timetable to arrive in Morpeth on Tuesday. The next day, we would get an idea of what the rain could do to them.

Sunday   Bendor to Glanton
"The next stopping places for the Wooler and Bendor route were Powburn, Glanton or Whittingham. By this time it was Sunday night, but we were not so far advanced in civilisation at that time as to pay much regard to the Fourth Commandment, and if at all remonstrated with in this respect, we very readily pleaded the works of necessity and mercy."

On Sunday morning, the drovers who had stayed at Bendor would round up the animals. They would pay the toll to pass through the gate, or organise a diversion to avoid it by backtracking from the inn, and heading over the floodplain of the River Glen, reaching Wooler without using the turnpike.

It would take three more days to reach Morpeth. The lanes along which Mary and I plan to follow south from Wooler cross several streams using fords, and as we make our way in the still pouring rain, we are not sure how easy it will be to get over them. It has rained all night, drenching summer rain. We are following the national cycle route 68 for the first few miles, covered head to toe in our waterproofs, and thinking about the drovers who had to keep to their timetable, regardless of the weather.

When we reach the first ford at Coldgate, the thundering, foaming brown water completely blocks the way. No motor vehicle can possibly get through, and we watch a car turning back. For us, there is a footbridge, which we cross, and go on. We are still on hard surfaced roads, following the cycle route. After South Middleton, the road becomes a track. The haugh beside the Lilburn stream would be so pretty in sunny weather, but today the burn is roaring tempestuously. We are blinded by the rain. To cross the burn, we have to tackle a steep slippery muddy bank down to the footbridge. Mary creeps down first, restraining her loaded bike, and mercifully doesn't slip. I take a blurry photograph of her, then do the same.

In the same circumstances, the drovers would have been soaked to the skin. We are overawed by their toughness, doing all this without waterproofs. Their woollen or linen clothing would have absorbed the water, and weighed heavily. Here is George Robson's account of flooding mountain streams:

> In a storm, when the mountain streams came down in torrents, it was a very trying and difficult time for us. We had often to wait for half a day until the small rivers subsided sufficiently to enable us to pass through sometimes with fifteen hundred sheep and lambs, and a hundred or two head of cattle. In order to get on we did not always wait till it was quite safe to pass them, and I have stood nearly up to my waist in the streams keeping the sheep and lambs from being carried down by the current.

> After being in water this way for a day or two together, we were, of course, as wet as water could make us, but we could get no change of clothes until we reached home four or five days afterward.

When he was interviewed at the age of eighty, he said that although he had a touch of rheumatism, "with such an experience, the wonder is that I am still here".

Folk Memory of Drovers going this Way

There is a misty folk memory of routes near Ilderton being drovers' tracks. Morag McMahon who lives in the village told me that her daughter had learned about it at school, but she was unable to substantiate it, and I couldn't track down the source. Similarly, octogenarian William Weddell from Haugh Head near Wooler said that his father told him the drovers used to cross the ford there. That could be a way to get back on to the turnpike just south of the toll gate at Haugh Head, to use the road without paying tolls. But it is all very vague. It is too long ago.

We squelch on to the hamlet of Ilderton, after which there is another muddy dene to manoeuvre down to the Roddam Burn. In spring, this lane is scented with primroses and bluebells, but now we push through soaking bracken, and cross the footbridge (NU 017204). A couple of young Romanian cyclists catch us up. They are following the national cycle route. Daniela said: "We read in the Lonely Planet guide that we would see lots of cyclists on this route. But you are the only people we have seen."

The way down to the ford is a classic holloway, a steep sided track, cut by the movements of animals over the passing of the years. Going up the other side, we just accept that our feet and bike wheels are deep in slithery mud.

The National Park Visitor Centre at Ingram is beckoning, where we can get a warm drink and a welcome from my friend who works there (NU 020163). Thankfully there is a bridge over the River Breamish. Mary and I strip off our soaking waterproofs and sink into the soft seats of the visitor centre. Sandra quizzes us about the state of the fords, so that she can tell other visitors. She puts on a DVD of the National Park Drovers Project. In 1943, farmer Bob Telford, from High Moralee at Wark, moved to Fawdon Farm near here, and walked his cattle the 45 miles between the two farms over the course of two days.

Alternative route from Ilderton to Brandon

From Ilderton, there are enticing minor roads, which are suitable for cyclists or walkers in good weather, heading south towards Brandon. Roseden Edge (NU 023215) is windy and open, with few hedges or walls, a reminder of what these grazing landscapes might have been like before the enclosures. A track leads past the oddly named Nova Scotia, over a burn with a meadow with a good watering place for animals. Old wayside stones and straggly hawthorns indicate that this is an ancient trackway.

The valley road away from Ingram goes through fine flat cycling country. In what is now merely a heavy drizzle, along by the brown roaring River Breamish, Mary and I follow the national cycle route which leads up the hill to Glanton Pike. We leave it and take the interestingly named West Turnpike Road to Glanton village.

It is still raining, although not so torrentially as before. We don't even consider sleeping in our tent, and we bang on the door of the Queen's Head in Glanton. We want to be like drovers, but as we are both 66 years old, we make excuses for ourselves. "Welcome ladies!" says the smiling owner of the inn, not looking at all disconcerted as water from our capes trickles all over his floor.

Monday morning   Glanton to Rimside Moor
"On the Monday morning, large quantities of sheep and cattle might be seen laid off for an hour's rest among the heather at the old inn and farmhouse on Rimside Moor, well kept by Mr and Mrs Wardle, while the drovers were supplied with a good breakfast."

George Robson's droving lanes to Morpeth now pass along one of the loveliest stretches of the road towards Rimside Moor. The rain-drenched landscape glitters in the morning sunlight. We are on the old turnpike now, part of the 1751 turnpike from Morpeth to Percy's Cross. We can picture the stage coaches and the horses as they struggle up the steep slopes towards us, the sound of the coachmen's horns, and the irritation at the delays when they encounter the long slow-moving droves of sheep and cattle.

George Robson and his drovers had stayed overnight at either Powburn, Glanton or Whittingham. Ian Roberts says: "A known drovers' inn at Whittingham is the Hole in the Wall – named after the method of serving drovers while keeping them outside the premises."[25] The old inn is now a private house.

In his book, Whittingham Vale, *David Dippie Dixon reports that the Hole-in-the-Wall was kept by Tom Dickinson in 1827, and he recorded this little ditty, p 181.*

If ever you go to Whittingham Fair,
  Be sure an' call at the 'Hole-in-the-Waa',
For there you get whisky for nowt
  An' brandy for nothing at aa'.

On the edge of Whittingham village, the former Castle Inn faced towards traffic arriving along the turnpike road from the south, and here the post horses were changed. As we leave the village, we spot the watering trough fed by a natural spring, which Ian Roberts points out as a feature of this droving route.[26]

Nowadays, the surfaced road comes to an end at Whittingham Lane farm. Mary and I push our bikes down to the old bridge over the little Swine Burn, which the coaches crossed in the turnpike days, and then up through dense grass and bluey-purple meadow cranesbill at the side of a field of peas. We nibble a few peas from the millions in the field.

Whichever way you go south from Whittingham towards Morpeth, the fell sandstone ridges of Thrunton and Rimside Moor have to be faced and crossed. We climb to the top of the hill past the forest car park, and look down over the next valley of the Coe Burn with the heights beyond. The scenery is breathtaking, even with the twentieth century pylons which cross it. The heathery slope up Rimside Moor beckons on the skyline. The stage and post coaches using the route found it notoriously difficult. The word roller-coaster probably wasn't invented then, but there is no better way to describe the road.

On the next incline up to Rough Castles are two embanked circular enclosures both marked as "camp" on the first edition 1860s Ordnance Survey map, and as "enclosure" on the modern ones. These are Iron Age defended settlements,[27] which Ian Roberts suggests may have been re-used as stock enclosures in the modern droving period.[28]

They are hauntingly beautiful in the morning light. Feeling sentimental, I think of the drovers herding their animals this way, resting there for a while after watering the cattle in the Coe Burn below, wondering who had built these evocative earthen rings, and why they were abandoned.

---

[25] Ian Roberts, p 116
[26] Ian Roberts, p 116
[27] www.keystothepast.info, N2757 and N2758
[28] Ian Roberts, p 116

There is an ancient wayside "stone" here, marked as such on the 1860s map (NU 091076). It could date back to the 1751 turnpike, or an even earlier time. It could also be some kind of boundary stone.

We push upwards along the narrow lane towards Rough Castles lined with creamy meadowsweet, pink rosebay willowherb and tumbling purple vetch, and find a roadside patch of purple spotted orchids. The heather-clad slopes of Rimside Moor lie ahead of us. On the skyline is a rounded clump of leaning beech trees, the breakfast destination for George Robson.

David Dippie Dixon and the old turnpike road

David Dippie Dixon was a local historian, who wrote the book Whittingham Vale *in 1895. He includes many anecdotes along this stretch of the old road. The Blackcock seems to be an area of land.*

> *The Blackcock, famous for the number and size of its adders, which infest the banks of the little burn whose waters flow from the Coe Crag eastward, through Thrunton Moor, is a piece of the wildest mountain scenery in the district. Here, early in the present century, there lived, in a miserable hovel, Jamie Macfarlane, a besom maker. Jamie had a daughter, Peggy, a very tall uncouth woman, who went about amongst the country folks selling the heather-besoms and scrubbers her father made. (p 158)*

> *During the great French War, when Bonaparte's threatened invasion was foremost in the thoughts of all England, and elaborate arrangements were made to meet the expected attack, Glanton was the centre fixed upon … for the volunteers in Glendate, Alndale and Upper Coquetdale … After a night of great excitement, authentic news arrived that the French had not landed, and that it had been a false alarm … Later in the afternoon, three Coquetdale Rangers, returning home to Rothbury, were crossing Rimside Moor, when they espied Jamie Macfarlane; whereupon they thought it would be a good joke to make Jamie believe they were French, and take him prisoner … They galloped across the moor with drawn swords towards poor Jamie; .. but as they approached him, he stooped down, and, looking through betwixt his legs, ran backwards towards them, shouting at the utmost pitch of his voice. The horses reared and plunged, and would on no account face the charge of Jamie Macfarlane.*

> *At which, the victorious Jamie shouted after them, "Hey! thre' bonny Sodgers, canna tyek a buzzum maker!" (p 248 – 249)*

One morning, poor Jamie Macfarlane was found dead in his hut on Thrunton Moor, and for several years after that, it was said that Jamie's ghost was always to be seen at midnight, with a "buzzom-shank over his shoulder". (p 159)

There is a story of a robbery along this road, in 1771. (p 299)

> *December 19th. Yesterday se'nnight, a woman going to Greenock was stopped, near Weldon Mill, in Northumberland, by a man and woman, and robbed of some money, after which they crammed her mouth with a handkerchief, tied it over with another, and her hands behind her back, then threw her into the ditch, where she was found almost suffocated by the landlord at Weldon Mill.*

This frightening story is also a comment on how poor people transported themselves. If you needed to go to Greenock, a couple of hundred miles from here, and you couldn't afford horse transport in any form, you simply walked. You took your chances, you set out, and you walked until you got there. Who was she, and why she was walking to Greenock in the winter time. Was it for work, or to visit her family? Was she destitute? Did she ever arrive, after the terrifying robbery?

Here is a story about the danger of the winter weather in this upland area in the year 1820. (p 306)

> *Mr Clement Stephenson, farmer, of Whittingham, and one of his men, were returning from Morpeth market where they had been with a drove of cattle. The day being stormy, they called for some refreshment at the beer shop, then kept by Jenny Knox, at Roughcastles. On coming out snow was falling very heavily, and on resuming their homeward journey, the two travellers came to where the road divided. Owing to the severity of the snowstorm, it was difficult to tell which was the right path. The man, thinking he was right, took one, and although he did his utmost to persuade his master to accompany him, Mr Stephenson, in the firm belief he was right, took the other, which unfortunately led into the midst of the wild moors of the Coe Crag and the Blackcock. Next day the body of Mr Stephenson was found in the snow, not far from Jamie Macfarlane's hut on Thrunton Moor.*

Twenty first century reality breaks into our musings. The old turnpike road here joins the modern A697. Speeding cars and thundering lorries now have to be faced for half a mile. There is no avoiding this unpleasant and dangerous part of the journey.

We arrive at the houses at the crossroads, the former Swinburne Arms. It is beautifully located, but the crossroads is dangerous. We follow the earlier turnpike up the stony byway to the beech trees at the top of the hill, to the site of the old inn.

From her inn, Mrs Wardle would hear the cattle, the dogs and the calling of the men, as they climbed the turnpike road between sheep-nibbled pasture and heather.

Here are the enclosures where George Robson told that the sheep and cattle might be laid off for an hour's rest. There is water available for them in the little burns running nearby.

To this day, the earthen paddocks remain, enclosing the century-old trees. Beyond the ruined inn is a crumbling but well-constructed stone bridge which was built for the turnpike road. On the other side of the bridge in the heathery moorland are large upright stones which look like gateposts for enclosures, now long gone. The old walls of the inn have recently been converted into sheep handling pens, with obvious remains of recent clipping, and this is where Mary and I get out the whisky bottle, the oatcakes and cheese for our lunch, and set up the self-timer to take a photo of ourselves.

It is the kind of place that makes one think of highwaymen, and ghostly stagecoaches. But probably it was just a busy inn, with hardworking country people earning some extra living from the regular drovers passing through.

We can guess what Mrs Wardle gave the drovers for breakfast. There is a description of the food eaten by the country people of Northumberland in Mackenzie's *Historical and Descriptive View of the County of Northumberland*, of 1811.

> In the north and west of Northumberland, bread is made of barley, or barley mixed with grey pease or beans ... it is kneaded with water, made into thin unleavened cakes and immediately baked on a girdle. Oatmeal also constitutes a principal article of food with the peasantry, not as bread, but in crowdies or hasty pudding, for breakfast; and sometimes for supper, eaten with butter or more commonly with milk.

In south Northumberland, they baked rye flour, or rye and wheat flours mixed together into *maslin*, formed cakes 1½ to 2 inches thick, and baked them in the oven.[29]

Mackenzie lamented the dram drinking and malt liquor, "a sottish habit to be much regretted". In case you might be thinking there is a typing error here, it is definitely a *sottish* habit he is talking about, rather than *Scottish*.

Changing names of the old inn on the moor

1769 Armstrong's map	*Halfway House*
1820 Fryer's map	*Rimpside Moor House*
1828 Greenwood's map	*Rimside Inn*
1860 first edition OS	*Moor House. The new inn at the crossroads is Swinburne Arms*
1898 second edition OS	*Old Moor House. The inn at the crossroads is now New Moor House.*

Halfway House probably means halfway between Morpeth and Wooler, and this can be seen from the mile stages on Armstrong's map. It is fifteen miles from Morpeth, and we have come nineteen from Cornhill. This agrees with George Robson's roughly one and a half days' droving from Bendor to this point, and the same lying ahead to Morpeth.

The first edition 1860s Ordnance Survey map shows some curious placenames here. There are two t-shaped enclosures nearby marked as *bield,* just beyond the inn. This is an old word for *shelter*, and still used with this meaning in the Scottish Borders. The fallen stone walls of one of them can just be seen on a small hill a little way beyond the inn. Sheep shelters are more usually the circular stells in Northumberland, but this t-shaped one is a rarity. Also, down the hill towards the A697 is a small building marked on the map as Wheatfold. This is just the foundations of a ruin now, but perhaps wheat was grown as a crop here in the nineteenth century.

The Wardles were a well established local family. Mrs Wardle is named on the 1841 census, aged 65, as a widow and innkeeper at Moor House. She was still there in 1851. Her son lived at the New Moor House inn, and was farming 1500 acres of land. When George Robson passed through, she would have been a busy middle-aged woman.

Monday, after breakfast
"Then the road was taken again through Long Framlingon, and that night's resting stations were Weldon Bridge and Longhorsley."

The road leaving the inn is a green moorland pathway, and it is a pleasure to walk barefoot on the sheep-cropped grass, just like the Highland drovers must have done.

There was a tollgate one and a half miles ahead, at Framlington Gate. Thomas Wardle was named as the farmer here in 1828.[30] Drovers who wanted to avoid the toll gate could divert around the side of Wooden Hill as they left the Rimside Inn, towards Shirlaw Hope, heading for Woodhead. This is what Mary and I do.

We push through the forest trails, and cross Shirlaw Hope burn. Willows and alders line the brown pools of the stream. Mackenzie tells us that at the bottom of Shirlaw Hope "issues a fine spring of water, the stream of which, with a little assistance, is powerful enough to turn the wheel of a corn mill."[31]

---

[29] E Mackenzie, vol 1, p 231
[30] Parson and White, p 473
[31] E Mackenzie, vol 1, p 706

Our path takes us through Longframlington Common, past the stone outline of an old cottage at Mount Pleasant and some stock enclosures. Now only a scraggly leaning hawthorn survives among the stones. There are ridge and furrow patterns in the fields below. Above us, marked on our map in Gothic script, are prehistoric cairns, a settlement and field system. Could any landscape be more enchanting on what is now a sunny summer day, with its layers of history?

But this is what Mackenzie has to say on the subject of Longframlington Common. "The soil is of an inferior quality, and, about eighty years ago, was covered with whins and heath, when a division of the best parts took place, leaving an oblong tract, consisting of about one thousand acres, of the wildest and most dreary moor-land in the county."

The wild and dreary moorland is what the drovers would have liked, as it is more likely to have allowed them unencumbered progress.

We struggle with our bikes along the bridle way through some deeply rutted fields, where progress is very difficult, doing our best to avoid the attentions of a herd of beef cows with an enormous bull.

Mackenzie also mentions that "about two miles north of the village, there are … a great number of cairns, scattered over several acres … Some are nine or ten feet high, others not more than three or four feet. Indeed, the situation in which they are placed is so remote, and the access to it so difficult, that very few people in the neighbourhood have either seen or heard of them."

As we climb a little higher, and pass round the curve of the hill, the view to the Simonside hills suddenly opens out to the west. Now we learn what Mackenzie was talking about. We find a prominent standing stone on a small hillock, and we head for it. It seems to be embedded in an ancient circle of stones, perhaps a Bronze Age field clearance or burial cairn. This surely is a landmark for the drovers. They would rest here, as we do, gazing over the last stretch of the way to Morpeth.

The ridges of land roll ahead in waves on the skyline, where hedgerows outline the pattern of the lanes we must follow. It is green, rich and mellow. The meandering line of trees down in the valley follows the River Coquet, waiting to be crossed. The skylarks are singing. The gorse is golden, among the greenery. The sea is on the far eastern horizon, and the dark Simonside hills to the west. Even here, we are aware of the former turnpike road, and we can see the movement of the big lorries to our left, moving between Scotland and England.

The next major event in the journey is the crossing of the River Coquet. On the last night before Morpeth, those who used the traditional ways before the bridge at Weldon was constructed needed to ford the river. Earlier delving in the Northumberland Archives had enabled me to locate the fords which local people used, and which drovers would have known about. The table of sources for this information is shown at the end of the chapter.

The map shows selected minor roads, bridle ways and footpaths which are still rights of way, and which led to fords over the River Coquet at the named dates. Drovers could have used these fords after coming over from Rimside Moor on their way to Morpeth. The only one of the fords which is still a right of way is the one near Middleheugh.

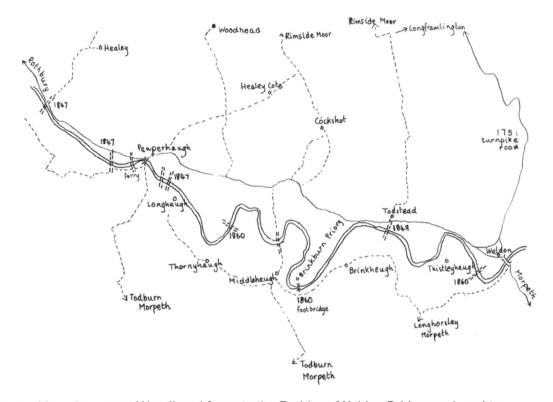

Mary and I go down past Woodhead farm, to the Rothbury/Weldon Bridge road, and to Middleheugh ford, but we can't cross it. The river is still high, after the rain. I've seen it after a dry spell, and even then I wouldn't dare to cross it.

It probably wouldn't have stopped the drovers, and they would see the ruined Brinkburn Priory on their left as they climbed the banks towards Middleheugh farmhouse.

Brinkburn Priory in 1840
From Hodgson's History of Northumberland

We are obliged to follow the main road to the Anglers' Arms at Weldon Bridge. For George Robson and his droves, this is the last night before they needed to arrive in Morpeth. The original bridge was built in 1744, and although it was washed away it was rebuilt in 1749 and 1752.[32] It is now bypassed by a 1960s bridge.

Tuesday   Weldon Bridge to Morpeth

"Next morning, Tuesday, the seven miles to Morpeth were easily performed, where the stock generally arrived between ten and twelve. They were then put into fields, and fed and rested until next morning, Wednesday, market day."

The lanes along the ridges between Weldon Bridge and Morpeth are lined with wild roses and honeysuckle. Chaffinches and yellowhammers are flying ahead of Mary and me as we make our way between the hedgerows of the enclosed fields. The lanes have wide verges, allowing grazing for the cattle as they passed along. George Robson and his drovers would be likely to meet others coming in from the Rothbury direction, as they made their way through this network. Sometimes the flocks and herds would come close to each other, and old acquaintances would surely be renewed.

Along the way, a few miles from Morpeth near Beacon Hill, there is an elevated patch of open land with gorse and bracken (NZ147921). From here, there is a view back towards Scotland, over the ridges of Longframlington Moor which we have just crossed, and the further Cheviots where other flocks and herds would be moving. There must have been moments when the drovers of old took a backward glance, just like we do, when we pause to lunch on our oatcakes. Like us, they'd be thinking about the way they'd come. And then they'd turn again to the last mile or two to the town.

One of the routes merging near Morpeth goes past Fairmoor. This is now a hamlet of fairly modern houses just south of the junction of the roads from Coldstream and Alnwick. It would have been an ideal location for the sale of large droves of animals coming for special fairs at Morpeth. It seems possible, from the place name, that fairs may have taken place here, although it is hard to find any definite evidence. Bailey and Culley's book, written in 1795 and reprinted in 1805, gives us some clues. They record an annual cattle and sheep fair on the Wednesdays before Whitsuntide, on the Wednesdays before the 22nd of July, for fat cattle, sheep etc.[33] Could the fairs have been held at Fairmoor?

Margaret Maddison used her research skills to help me here:

> The Fair Moor ceased to exist when it was enclosed and divided up in 1799. I have records of allotments made in 1799, as a result of this. One of these was Spring Gardens at the north end of Morpeth. So no fair could have been held there after 1798.

She found records of crimes committed at Cowhill Fair in 1715 and 1717. Although I haven't found anyone who knows where Cowhill was, it could have been at this location.

Relying on this shaky evidence, it is possible that George Robson would have attended events at Fairmoor in his younger days.

We've come a long way with George Robson, his companions and his animals, on his five day drove from Coldstream to Morpeth. There must always have been a sense of satisfaction at the journey safely accomplished. Soon, they would be putting the animals in the holding fields, and enjoying the convivial inns with their friendly widows.

---

[32] Robert Robson, p 66
[33] J Bailey and B Culley, p 172

Wingates Droving Road

Among the network of lanes between Weldon Bridge and Morpeth is the township of Wingates. Before the rise of motor traffic, the animals would be driven on foot.

A traditional way to drive animals can be identified from East Wingates heading for Morpeth. It goes past Wingates Wholme farm, from where a clear holloway leads down to the surfaced road. After following the hard road for half a mile, the old droving route went straight on, but if you are driving a car, you must turn right or left. For some reason, the authorities chose not to continue making the hard road to Morpeth here. The direct droving route thus goes straight on. Passing the house at High Southward Edge, it crosses the Devil's Causeway and follows a field. Soon, a wide track can be seen, running between earthen banks 15 – 17 yards apart, with hedgerow trees still standing. It is shown as this wide track as far back as the first edition 1860s Ordnance Survey map. A public footpath follows it to this day, although it is difficult to penetrate in places owing to gorse and bog. It is shown on the Ordnance Survey Explorer map 325 with the same wide boundaries, the best stretch being from NZ 130933 to NZ 138931.

Once on the hard road again, the route heads in a straight line for Heighley Gate and Morpeth.

Sources for location of fords between Healey and Weldon Bridge

near Healey, ford	1847 The Raw Tithe Plan
Pauperhaugh, three fords and a ferry	1847 Pauperhaugh Tithe Plan
Pauperhaugh Bridge	1862
near Thorneyhaugh, ford	1860s Ordnance Survey
Middleheugh, ford	1844 Brinkburn High Ward Tithe Plan
near Brinkburn, footbridge	1860s Ordnance Survey
Todstead, ford	1849 Brinkburn Low Ward Tithe Plan
near Thistleyhaugh, ford	1860s Ordnance Survey

Drovers arriving at Framlington Gate toll bar, 1800

George Robson makes it clear that drovers avoided the expense of turnpike roads if they could. They were people with freedom and adventure in their nature, who needed unimpeded access across hill and vale in order to move great herds of cattle and flocks of sheep for tens, even hundreds, of miles. This had always been the case. In prehistoric times, hunter gatherers had followed wild animals to kill them for food. After domestication of wild animals, the early farmers moved their cattle and sheep to and from the pastures, according to the season. In historic times, cattle thieves used the border tracks, and legitimate traders required free movement for their animals along the roads to market. We have direct evidence that in the seventeenth century, Scottish cattle were being brought to Morpeth. But by the time George Robson was droving, things had begun to change.

Until 1747, drovers and other travellers could use the roads without charge whichever way they came to Morpeth. They might have had to put up with filthy, rutted tracks, floods, ice and snow, or fallen branches, but they didn't need to pay.

Here is a description of the state of the roads at that time. Written about Scotland, it is likely to be very similar in much of Northumberland. "The highways were tracks of mire in wet weather and marshes in summer till the frosts made them sheets of ice covered with drifting snow. When rain fell, the flat ground became lakes with islands of stone and the declavities became cataracts. Even towns were often connected by nothing more than pack roads on which horses stumbled perilously along and carriages could not pass at all, over unenclosed land and moorland where, after rain, it was difficult to trace any beaten track."[34]

A road at High Rochester, Redesdale, Northumberland, 1827

From Hodgson's History of Northumberland

Since 1553, parishes throughout England and Wales had been responsible for the upkeep of the roads within their boundaries. Parishioners were required to spend four, and later six days, labouring to repair the roads, and this was not a popular duty. Landowners increasing their production during the agricultural improvements of the eighteenth and early nineteenth century wanted to get their goods and livestock to market. Lime and manure needed to be carted to the newly enclosed fields. Something had to be done.

By the mid 1700s, turnpike trusts were being set up by groups of influential landowners. They would seek an act of Parliament to enable them to raise funds to build a good quality road upon which tolls would be paid by road users. In this way they would maintain the road and repay the original investment. The so-called Turnpike Mania took place between 1751 and

---

[34] H G Graham, *Life of Scotland in the Eighteenth Century,* quoted in John James Mackay, p 39

1772. By the latter date, Morpeth was the focus of several turnpike roads. This went hand in hand with the expansion of the town's fatstock market.

The first turnpike passed through Morpeth in 1747, from Newcastle in the direction of Berwick. Next was the road through Longhorsley towards Wooler as far as Percy's Cross, in 1751. In the same year, the Morpeth to Elsdon turnpike trust was established. The Morpeth to North Shields turnpike trust followed later in 1814.[35]

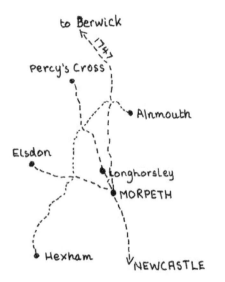

Roads turnpiked in Morpeth area by 1752

Adapted from William Albert p 50

As Sir Walter Scott wrote, the drovers "are required to know perfectly the drove-roads, which lie over the wildest tracts of the country, and to avoid as much as possible the highways, which distress the feet of the bullocks, and the turnpikes, which annoy the spirit of the drover."

Every time the drovers passed through the gates, they had to pay tolls per score of animals. Naturally they did not like doing this. There was often a decision to be made. Going along the turnpikes might be quicker and more direct. There would be bridges over the rivers, and inns along the way. But there were disadvantages too. As well as having to pay onerous tolls, the hard surfaces of the turnpike roads "distressed the feet of the bullocks". It could even mean that the cattle needed to be shoed, an expensive and time-consuming process. The herds could delay post coaches, and annoy other travellers.

Drovers were not exempted from tolls like other more fortunate groups. It will not surprise us to learn that those exempted included the royal family, people on their way to church on Sundays or to funerals, and the military. Other exemptions were carriages during elections, the post, and carts with manure, agricultural implements or goods not going to market. The last mentioned would include local farming people going about their everyday business.

The drovers however had to pay. At a typical payment of between six and ten pence per score of cattle, their passing through the gates was income for the trustees. But if it was practical for them to choose a route which avoided the toll gates, they would often do so. Even if they had to use the turnpikes, they would frequently find ways to avoid paying at the gates.

There is an account of Scottish drovers passing along the Great North Road, in Gainsborough, Lincolnshire. "We have often been amused while witnessing the 'haggling' between some Scottish drover and an English gatekeeper. Sandy endeavours to drive his cattle through as quick as he can, so as to confuse the toll-man while keeping count; and ere they have settled the dispute the drove is half-a-mile ahead, and another drove fast approaching the gate."[36]

---

[35] William Albert, pp 50 – 51
[36] William Thompson, p 180

Sometimes drovers would circle around the gates and return to the turnpike further on. Another account tells us that "it was difficult to check effectively all the ingenious methods involved". Trustees of a road near Wakefield in Yorkshire complained in 1758, that "there are some who ride thro' the River Calder at Sunset to save their penny, such sordid dogs dwell in this Country".[37]

The turnpike road network was developing in the context of relations between Scotland and England, after the crushing of the Jacobite rebellions in 1745. People living in Morpeth were close to these events, and would be aware that there was an ever present danger of further civil war. The government was enabling construction of roads and bridges for better communications. There were several turnpike acts formed in 1762 in the Coldstream area, and the bridge over the River Tweed was completed by 1766.[38] Until that time, armies and drovers had had to ford the Tweed, which they could do at Coldstream.[39]

After 1785, there was a daily stage coach service between Edinburgh and Morpeth along this route. This does not automatically mean that the road had become excellent. As Richard Carlton's encyclopaedic report on cross-border roads points out, "the system on both sides of the border remained free from central planning, therefore rather piecemeal in nature, each new section being created for reasons of local interest ... Indeed it is important to bear in mind that the act of turnpiking does not necessarily imply road improvement... still less frequently the construction of a new road, merely the intention to maintain and improve an existing road. Nor does it necessarily imply that wheeled transport was predominating on all routes, since transportation by pack-horse and droving continued."[40]

The road between Coldstream and Morpeth is now the heavily used A697. In the past, it was turnpiked at different times along three stretches, between 1751 and 1884 when the last turnpike trust closed. Drovers and other travellers would constantly have needed to adapt to the changes as they occurred.

1751	Breamish Turnpike Trust	From near Morpeth to Percy's Cross
1792	Ford and Lowick Trust	Cornhill to Milfield Burn
1806	Wooler Turnpike Trust	Percy's Cross to Milfield Burn
1831	Wooler & Breamish Turnpike Trust	amalgamation of Breamish and Wooler trusts

The toll gates with their cottage were rented out on an annual basis, as these advertisements from the Newcastle Courant show.

1805	The Breamish Turnpike Road (Trust)
Powburn Gate	£177
Framlington Gate	£172
High Laws Gate	£190

1820	The Breamish Turnpike Road (Trust)
Powburn Gate	£190
Framlington Gate	£172
High Laws Gate	£161

1835	Wooler and Breamish Turnpike Road (Trust)
Bender Gate	£340
Haughhead Gate	£254
Doddington Gate	£250
Powburn Gate	£251
Framlington Gate	£250
Heighlaws Gate	£410

[37] William Albert, p 82
[38] John James Mackay, p 45
[39] Ian Roberts, pp 113 - 114
[40] Richard Carlton, 2009, p 30

The map below shows the location of the toll gates on these early turnpike roads. While there is no trace of these gates now, two are remembered by their still surviving names, Heighley Gate and Framlington Gate. When I realised the fact that the place names actually referred to toll gates I was quite surprised that I had never made the connection.

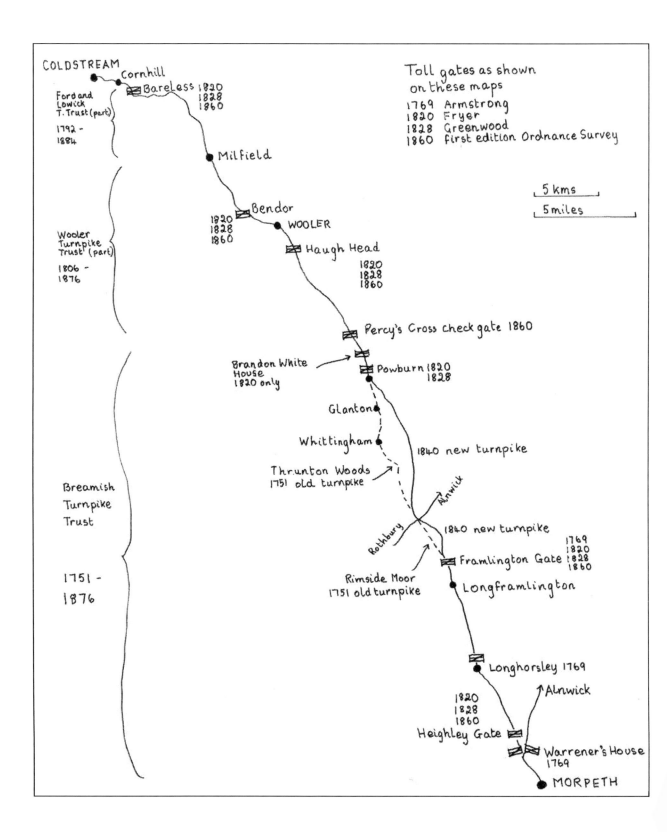

COLDSTREAM
Cornhill
Bareless 1820
1828
1860
Ford and
Lowick
T. Trust (part)

1792 -
1884

Toll gates as shown
on these maps
1769 Armstrong
1820 Fryer
1828 Greenwood
1860 first edition Ordnance Survey

5 kms
5 miles

Milfield

Wooler
Turnpike
Trust (part)

1806 -
1876

Bendor
1820
1828
1860
WOOLER
Haugh Head
1820
1828
1860

Percy's Cross check gate 1860

Brandon White
House
1820 only
Powburn 1820
1828

Breamish
Turnpike
Trust

Glanton

Whittingham
1840 new turnpike

Thrunton Woods
1751 old turnpike

Alnwick

Rothbury
1840 new turnpike
1769
1820
Framlington Gate 1828
1860

1751 -

1876

Rimside Moor
1751 old turnpike
Longframlington

Longhorsley 1769

1820
1828
1860
Heighley Gate

Alnwick

Warrener's House
1769

MORPETH

36

The examples of charges to be paid, shown below, are taken from the 1751 Longhorsley to Percy Cross Turnpike Act for the Breamish Turnpike Road.

> For every Horse, Mare, Gelding, Mule, Ass, or Beast of Burden, laden or unladen, and not drawing, the Sum of Three Pence.
>
> For every Drove of Oxen or Neat Cattle, the Sum of Ten Pence per Score; and so in Proportion for any greater or lefs Number.
>
> For every Drove of Calves, Swine, Sheep, Lambs, or Goats, the Sum of Five Pence per Score; and so in Proportion for any greater or lefs Number.

"For every Horse, Mare, Gelding, Mule, Ass, or Beast of Burden, laden or unladen, and not drawing, the Sum of Three Pence

"For every Drove of Oxen or Neat Cattle, the Sum of Ten Pence per Score; and so in Proportion for any greater or less Number

"For every Drove of Calves, Swine, Sheep, Lambs, or Goats, the Sum of Five Pence per Score; and so in Proportion for any greater or less Number."[41]

We can get a very rough idea of the great expense for the drovers by calculating the value of ten pence in 1751 with present day prices. Using an inflation and price converter website, it works out at approximately £17 for a score of cattle.[42] According to Armstrong's map there were three turnpike gates along this turnpike road at that time. If the drover had one hundred cattle, it would cost roughly £85 per gate, and £255 by today's prices to pass the three gates.

By 1820, the renewal act for the same turnpike trust is charging six pence for every score of oxen, cows, calves or other neat cattle, and three pence for every score of hogs, swine, goats, sheep or lambs. The prices have gone down. This act states that tolls are only to be charged once a day for the same animals, and that only three full tolls are to be taken along the length of the said road in any twenty four hours.[43]

In the 1807 turnpike act for the road between Percy's Cross and Milfield Burn, the tolls are six pence per score for oxen, and one shilling and two pence (ie 14 pence) per score for calves, hogs, sheep or lambs.

Why the toll for calves should be more than twice as costly was puzzling. The mystery was solved at a very late stage in writing this text, when I was looking again at the turnpike acts in Newcastle City Library. Lo and behold, there was also an 1808 turnpike act for the Percy Cross to Milfield Burn road, only a year after the previous one. As there were usually 25 years or so between acts, this was rather surprising. I checked the tolls. In 1808, the tolls for a score of oxen had been negotiated downwards to five pence, but that for calves, hogs, sheep and lambs down to twopence ha'penny. In other words, there had been a mis-print by the House of Commons, which no-one had noticed! We can imagine the furore this must have caused in Northumberland at the toll gates.[44]

Generally, evasion of paying the tolls had become an issue of such importance to the trustees that by the time of the 1820 Longhorsley to Percy Cross renewal act, there was a fine of up to five pounds for evasion. This applied to both the guilty persons who "pass through any land or

---

[41] Longhorsley to Percy Cross turnpike act 1751
[42] safalra.com/other/historical-uk-inflation-price-conversion
[43] Longhorsley to Percy Cross turnpike renewal act 1820
[44] Percy Cross to Milfield Burn turnpike act 1807

grounds lying near any Turnpike or Toll Gate", or "any Owner or Occupier of such Lands" who permits such persons to pass through.

Successive turnpike acts would renew the conditions, and review the tolls charges, sometimes making minor route changes as well.

There is no living memory of these old turnpike roads, but now let's make a journey from Cornhill to Morpeth, seeing the route as the drovers would have done, and finding out what can still be seen to this day.

From Cornhill to Percy's Cross

The first important feature the drovers would have met after leaving Cornhill was the toll gate just beyond Bareless Farm, at the junction in the road towards East Learmouth (NT 877383). No sign of it exists today. There is not even a place name to remind us.

After negotiating the toll bar at Bareless, the drovers would pass a standing stone in a field opposite Crookham Westfield farm, marked on the modern map as The King's Stone (NT 884383). It is a prehistoric stone, but was traditionally believed to mark the spot where James IV of Scotland was killed at the Battle of Flodden.[45] In the earlier droving days, it is the kind of landmark that would help drovers stay on the right route.

The road then passes by Pallinsburn House, with its parks, lakes and woodland, and its lodge on the main road. Ian Roberts tells us that "the rich arable land of this district was the site of early attempts to intensify agricultural production, and went hand in hand with improvements to the road following turnpiking in the 1760s. The Blue Bell at Pallinsburn, near Crookham, is a former coaching inn associated with the turnpike, while the nearby Coach House hotel is an earlier place of rest which may have been used by drovers as well as coaches, perhaps as an intermediate rest station if not for overnight stops."[46]

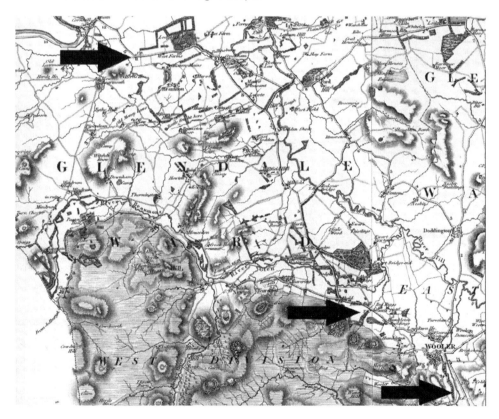

Map reproduced with permission of the Craster family

---

[45] Richard Carlton, Appendix 1, A 697 site no 192
[46] Ian Roberts, p 114

These extracts from Greenwood's 1828 map show three toll bars marked as TB, at Bareless just beyond Cornhill, the Black Bull at Akeld, and Haugh Head just south of Wooler.

Many of the features which the drovers would have seen are shown on the first edition 1860s Ordnance Survey map at Northumberland Archives in Woodhorn. A smithy is marked at Pallinsburn, two wells - Dorothy's Well just south of Crookham village itself, and another at the junction of the road to Ford. The River Till runs very close to the road here, which could have provided a suitable midday watering point for large herds. Milfield also has a couple of wells marked, and a smithy.

At Bendor, the Black Bull Inn where George Robson and the drovers stayed is marked on the 1860s map, and so is the standing stone in the nearby field. Although it is named as the Battle Stone, and is traditionally associated with the 1402 Battle of Homildon Hill, it is actually a Bronze Age standing stone (NT 968294).

Just past Bendor, there are two alternative roads into Wooler. The older road reaches the High Street, with its former coaching inns, including another named the Black Bull, "standing on the edge of the market place, first recorded in 1199."[47]

In the early nineteenth century, Wooler was a busy market town, and Pigot's Directory of 1822 lists eleven taverns. The Tankerville Arms in 1822 was an inn acting as a posting and excise centre, managed by Alex McGregor.

The Wellington coach from Newcastle called there every day at half past twelve, on its way to Coldstream and Edinburgh. At three every afternoon, the coach called in on its way to Newcastle through Glanton and Morpeth. It is undoubtedly the case that the drovers would have had to manoeuvre their animals around the coach because they encountered it twice daily along the turnpike road. There was also the constant movement of carriers and their carts. Pigot's Directory lists regular services every weekday between Wooler and Coldstream, and from there through Glanton to Morpeth and Newcastle.[48]

Leaving Wooler, the next toll gate is just to the south of the town, at Haugh Head, where the toll cottage still survives. A milepost on the left hand side of the road shows 30 miles to Morpeth, 317 miles to London, 14 to Cornhill and 61 miles to Edinburgh.

The toll cottage at Haugh Head. The small window by the roadside would be used to observe the approaching droves.

---

[47] Ian Roberts, p 115
[48] Pigot's Directory for Northumberland, p 624

Ian Roberts points out: "After Haugh Head, the road passes through a landscape dominated by features of nineteenth-century estate farms and country houses which grew from the profits of agricultural improvement, aided by developments in transport, particularly the turnpikes and railways."[49] Dunny's Well, just over a mile beyond the Haugh Head toll gate, is marked on old OS maps. It is still there, rather filled up now with waterside plants. This could have been a midday watering point between Bendor and the evening stop at Powburn or Glanton.

The turnpike road now approaches another easy-to-miss feature, but a very important one after 1751. Just south of what is now Scott's sawmills, on the left hand side of the road is an old-fashioned stone cottage, with a small walled garden in front, and outbuildings behind (NU 050194).

The cottage appears on the first edition 1860s Ordnance Survey map next to what is called a Check Gate. It is at the northern end of the first 1751 Longhorsley to Percy's Cross turnpike road, of the Breamish Turnpike Trust. It seems an odd place, in the middle of nowhere special, to start or end a turnpike road. The reason was probably related to landownership, as two great estates came together at this point - Lilburn to the north and Hedgeley to the south.

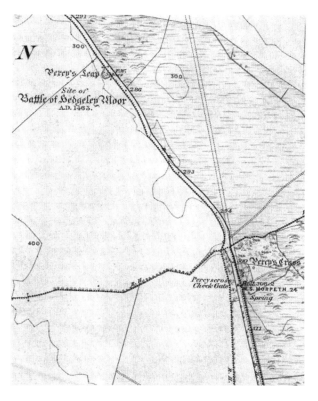

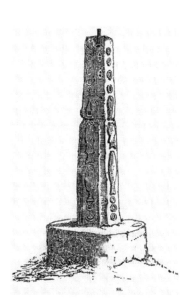

This extract is from the first edition 1860s Ordnance Survey map. It shows the Check Gate at Percy's Cross and the old milestone, Morpeth 24.
Reproduced with permission of Northumberland Archives

Nowadays, there is no sign of the Check Gate.

The curiously carved Percy's Cross is just behind the cottage. It is a memorial to Sir Ralph Percy, who died nearby in the 1464 Battle of Hedgeley Moor. The cross "has been mistaken for a Roman milestone, but it is really a 15th century sandstone pillar with the stars and crescents of the Percies profusely carved upon it." The drawing above is from Edmund Bogg's book of 1898. The site is worth a visit, but as the road nowadays is busy, parking needs to be done with care, near the cottage.

---

[49] Ian Roberts, p 115

On the other side of the road, a little further north, there is another monument to Percy. "He is commemorated by a cross, and by two mossy stones invested with legend. The stones are known as Percy's Leap, and are in a little walled tree-shaded enclosure beside the main road. They are nine yards apart, and are said to mark the long leap that Percy took on receiving his mortal wound."[50]

Mileposts from Cornhill to Percy's Cross
As the travellers along this road made their way south from Cornhill, they would have been able to mark their progress by the roadside milestones and mileposts. Mileage as a concept was perhaps something relatively new. Distance in those days was more likely to be measured in time, rather than miles; four days' driving cattle from Cornhill to Morpeth would be more meaningful than 44 miles.

The turnpike acts made it compulsory to place milestones, or mileposts made of metal, showing distances to important towns. The 1751 Longhorsley to Percy Cross Act states that the trustees "are hereby required to cause the said Road to be measured, and Stones or Posts to be thereon … at the Distance of One Mile from another, and denoting the Distance of every Stone or Post from any other Place."

Any person who "shall maliciously break any of the Stones or Posts" or "shall obliterate or deface any of the Words, Letters, Figures or Marks, which shall be engraved thereon" would be liable to pay the fine of forty shillings.[51]

The table on the next page shows the mileposts between Cornhill and Percy's Cross. I've recorded them in the order in which the drovers would have found them, from north to south, as they used the turnpike from Scotland towards Morpeth.

In case you would like to look for them, the table excludes missing mileposts, even though they may be marked on modern maps. These are all now officially protected Grade II listed buildings. They all follow the same format, and an example is shown the photo. They show the distance to Morpeth and London going south, and to Cornhill and Edinburgh going north.

Milestone information in this study was obtained with the help of Iain Davison, the local active member of the Milestone Society.
Photo: Iain Davison

---

[50] Northumberland Education Committee, p 298
[51] Longhorsley to Percy Cross Turnpike Act, 1751

Mor 41, L 328, Cor 3, E 50	¼ mile S of Pallinsburn House, N of road	NT 896365
Mor 40, L 327, Cor 4, E 51	opposite Blue Bell inn, N of road	NT 911382
Mor 39, L 326, Cor 5, E 52	220 yds W of Mount Pleasant, E of road	NT 921370
Mor 38, L 325, Cor 6, E 53	just N of junction with B6352, E of road	NT 930358
Mor 36, L 323, Cor 8, E 55	¾ mile S of Milfield, E of road	NT 941330
Mor 35, L 322, Cor 9, E 56	220 yds N of Ewart Park W Lodge, E of road	NT 949312
Mor 32, L 319, Cor 12, E 59	E of Humbleton Buildings, N of road	NT 981289
Mor 31, L 318, Cor 13, E 60	in Wooler, re-sited	NT 993282
Mor 30, L 317, Cor 14, E 61	Haugh Head toll cottage	NU 001267
Mor 28, L 315, Cor 16, E 63	just S of Dunny's Well	NU 016240
old unmarked stone	Percy's Cross cottage	NU 050197

The old stone outside Percy's Cross Cottage probably pre-dates the later metal mileposts. On the first edition 1860s Ordnance Survey map, it is marked as Morpeth 24. It doesn't quite tally with the mileage on the metal milepost a quarter of a mile to south of it, which is marked as 24 miles to Morpeth.

It could therefore be part of an older system, possibly dating from the 1751 turnpike which ended here. The Wooler and the Breamish turnpike trusts amalgamated in 1831. The trustees may have decided it was time to upgrade an old-fashioned system. (By the time of the second edition 1899 Ordnance Survey map, this stone is marked as Old MS, with no sign of the Check Gate, as the road was no longer a toll road.)

The old milestone at Percy Cross cottage

Percy's Cross cottage to Morpeth
From Percy's Cross cottage, the road follows the Devil's Causeway for a few miles. This connected the Roman settlements at Berwick and Corbridge, and on Armstrong's 1769 map, it is still shown as a significant route. Nowadays, although marked on maps, there is little trace to be seen on the ground. It is possible that the early drovers along this way might have been aware of the Devil's Causeway, and that it was a Roman road in origin. This dead straight stretch of road is just how we imagine Roman roads to be.

Further along, the Fryer and Greenwood maps of 1820 and 1828 show toll gates at Brandon White House and Powburn. The toll gates that the drovers encountered would have been dependant on the exact dates of their journeys.

The next three villages of Powburn, Glanton or Whittingham are places where George Robson records that the drovers would stay on Sunday night. Pigot's 1822 Directory tells us that at Powburn, there was a blacksmith named Robert Brown, and an inn called The Plough. In Glanton, there was a blacksmith called Ralph Coxon, and the inns were the Red Lion and the Nag's Head. Whittingham had the Castle posting inn, run by Daniel Ross.[52]

At Powburn, there is a significant y-junction, where the present-day A697 is the left fork, and a lesser road is to the right. Until the late 1830s, the right fork was the turnpike road. It headed up the hill towards Glanton, and on to Whittingham. It then went over the roller coaster of Thrunton and Rimside Moor, described by Mackenzie in 1811: "It climbs the long steep side of Rimside Hill ... all the advantages of a lower route having been abandoned in order to save the expense of building a bridge."[53] The time had come to put the problem right, and create an alternative route.

This was partly the result of discussions taking place at a national level, about creating more efficient post routes between London and Edinburgh. The road from Morpeth to Coldstream was on one of the main routes to Scotland. The Breamish and the Wooler turnpike trusts were preparing for amalgamation in the 1820s and 1830s, and trustees decided to create a new road to avoid the difficulties of Rimside Moor, along the stretch between Longframlington and Powburn. The table below summarises the changes.

1752	The original Breamish turnpike road crossed the difficult Rimside Moor and Thrunton roads, between Longframlington and Powburn.
1822	Thomas Telford was commissioned to survey the route from London to Edinburgh, including the route from Morpeth to Coldstream, and this stretch between Longframlington and Powburn. He chose a route to the east of Rimside Moor and Thrunton, closer to Edlingham. His route was never adopted.[54]
1831	James Cunningham was commissioned to survey a new road between Longframlington and Powburn. He estimated it would take two years from commencement to build, and the cost would be £11,921. This route was adopted, and the present A697 follows this course.[55]

By 1840, the new section of the turnpike road was completed. On the plan in the Longframlington Township Tithe Award of 1844, the point where the old and the new turnpikes come together at its southern end is clearly shown, at Framlington Gate (NU 118037), and the toll bar remained in the same location.[56]

---

[52] Pigot's Directory for Northumberland, 1822, p 624
[53] E Mackenzie, Vol I, p 704
[54] Commons Report on Morpeth and Edinburgh Road, 1822, NRO 530.15/63 64
[55] James Cunningham, Map Present and Proposed Lines of Road from Powburn to Weldon Bridge
[56] Longframlington Township Tithe Award 1843, DT 303M

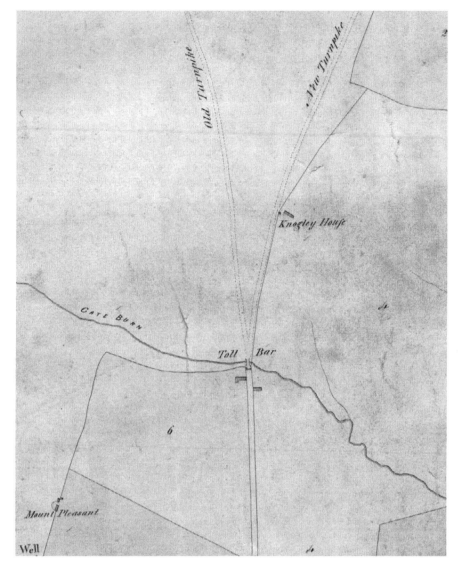

Junction of the old and new turnpikes at Framlington Gate, shown on the Longframlington 1844 tithe award

Map reproduced with permission of the Diocese of Newcastle upon Tyne

The toll bar at Framlington Gate remained in the same location throughout.

Continuing south, the road then passed the Besom Inn on the way to Longframlington village, an important stopping point. The 1828 Parson and White directory lists five inns. They were the Nag's Head at Low Framlington run by Ralph Bickerton; The Queen's Head by Robert Fail; The Turk's Head by John Hindhaugh; the New Inn by Ann Trewhitt, and the Horse and Jockey by Alder Gibson. Also, there were three smithies, run by Robert Carr, Thos. Gibson and Robt. Snowdon.

The old turnpike then winds round to the east of the present A697, over Roulands Bridge, to Weldon Bridge. Parson and White calls this "a small village and a commodious inn". The Angel Inn was run by Robert Richardson, and there was a blacksmith called Michael Watson.[57] Nowadays, it is the Anglers' Inn, and this is a good place to park and look for the milepost on the course of the old turnpike road.

---

[57] Parson and White directory, pp 456 - 473

Mileposts from Percy's Cross to Morpeth

Between Percy's Cross and Morpeth, the mileposts change their format. They are of a more sophisticated design than those of the Wooler Turnpike Trust further north, even though the more southerly part of the route was established earlier. They were made by the Smith Patterson iron foundry at Blaydon, as can be read on the moulded stem.

A Smith Patterson milepost
near Weldon Bridge

The table below shows the Smith Patterson mileposts that have survived between Percy's Cross and Longhorsley.

Cornhill 20, Morpeth 24, W 7	S of Percy's Cross	NU 055187
Cornhill 22, Morpeth 22, W 9	S of Powburn	NU 069161
Cornhill 23, Morpeth 21, W 10	between Glanton road ends	NU 077148
Cornhill 26, Morpeth 18, W 13	High Learchild	NU 094103
Cornhill 29, Morpeth 15, W 16	SE of New Moor House crossroads	NU 104060
Cornhill 32, Morpeth 12, W 19	near Besom Barn, damaged	NU 123022
Cornhill 33, Morpeth 11, W 20	in Longframlington village	NU 132009
Cornhill 35, Morpeth 9, W 22	S of Anglers' Arms, on old road	NU 139983
Cornhill 36, Morpeth 8, W 23	Bellamour, top of hill	NU 142967
Cornhill 38, Morpeth 6, W 25	S of Longhorsley, Whemley Burn	NU 156939

From the Angel Inn at Weldon Bridge, the traffic would be intensifying as drovers and travellers from other routes approached Morpeth, and where inns and smithies were located to provide their services. The 1769 Armstrong map shows a toll gate at Longhorsley, but this had disappeared by the time of the 1820 Fryer map. The OS map of 1860 shows a smithy, and two public houses, the Black Bull and the Star. Further on, there is another smith at Linden Square.

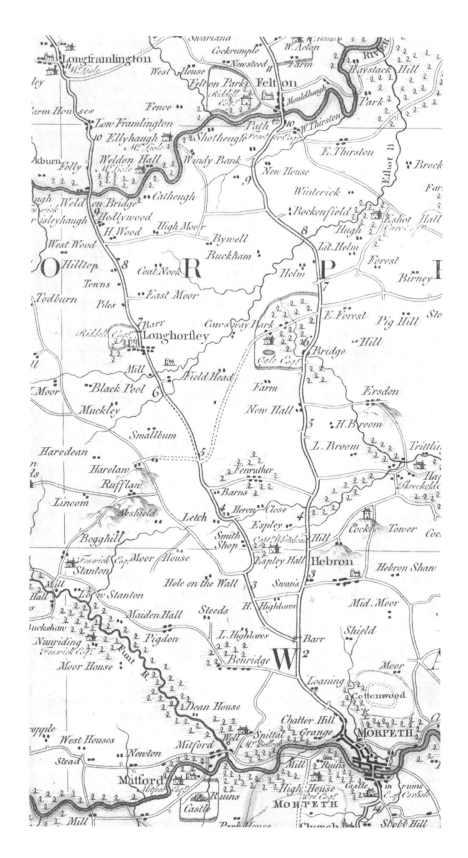

Armstrong's map of 1769 shows the double toll gates, marked Barr, just north of Morpeth where the turnpike roads to Alnwick and Percy's Cross separate. It also shows the toll gate at Longhorsley.

Reproduced with permission of Northumberland Archives

A mile from Morpeth, drovers who had used the turnpike from Coldstream would now be merging with those from Berwick and Alnwick, at Heighley Gate. The earlier gate had been at Warrener's house, which is shown on the Armstrong map above. The toll gate keepers must have been kept busy as the droves passed through the two gates, and the animals were moved down in their hundreds, even their thousands as they made their way to Morpeth.

Lying against the grassy bank, on the other side of a ditch where the blue dots of forget-me-nots pattern the grass, is a big grey stone. The word *Kelso* is engraved sharply on it, and the number 15. Mary and I drop our bikes and go to look.

This took place in the summer of 2010, long before I'd ever thought about writing this book. Meeting the milestone was an eye-opener. It is close to the dead end of the surfaced road leading south from Kelso to the Cheviots, on the road which stops at Cocklawfoot farm. Farmers from Cocklawfoot didn't need to know how far it was to Kelso. The milestone wasn't carved for them. It could only mean one thing. In the past, the route over the Cheviots must have been sufficient of a main road to require properly made milestones. But now, Clennell Street, as it is called, is only suitable for hikers who don't mind getting wet, mountain bikers who can bounce over the rocky sections, or riders on horses which pick their way through the difficult stretches. It is a wonderful, challenging and exciting path, but it isn't a road which needs carefully carved milestones.

What I have found out since then is that indeed Clennell Street was an important main route, and has been for hundreds, indeed thousands, of years. Even more interestingly, Iain Davidson, the Milestone Man, pointed me to Alastair Moffat's book *The Reivers*, which says that H for Harbottle and 11 was engraved on the back of this milestone.[58] Mary and I hadn't seen it because that side of the milestone was deeply embedded in the roadside bank. If true, it had great significance. Drovers and other travellers from the north were heading for the next important place, Harbottle, on the other side of the Cheviots.

While preparing for this book, I contacted the Scottish Borders Council's senior access officer, Neil Mackay. He arranged for his colleagues to locate the milestone and re-set it. Now everyone can see that it is 11½ miles to Harbottle, along Clennell Street. It is a real reminder of travellers who passed this way when it was one of the main routes between Scotland and England.

2010
The milestone stuck in the bank

2011
The other side of the re-instated milestone

We know from other sources that Clennell Street used to be a real and important drovers' route all the way to Morpeth. George Robson described it in the 1850s interview as one which avoided the turnpike gates. Even further back, in 1755, General Roy produced maps as part

---

[58] Alistair Moffat, p 43

of his Military Survey, and there we can see the route inscribed the *Road from Mopeth to Kelfo,* as it crosses the Border.[59]

In the first edition 1860s Ordnance Survey map, Clennell Street is shown as one of several Border crossings through the Cheviots.

Nowadays, when we are in Morpeth thinking about Kelso, it feels a long way away, with the barrier of the Cheviots in between. To get there by road, we need to drive round the hills to the east, or cross them to the west via Carter Bar. But in the eighteenth century, it seems, the most direct way to get there was to head along Clennell Street, on foot or horseback. There would have been a network of business connections between the towns.

Only just within living memory, the stories becoming more and more vague as the older generation pass on, people moved over these hills in the normal course of their lives. Barry Tomas lives in Alwinton and told me this story. His great auntie was a dealer, in the late nineteenth century and first decades of the twentieth. After lambing was over, in the spring, she would move around the many tracks in the hills with her packhorses, delivering goods, and picking up other goods to sell. She would trade in corn, blankets, cloth flour, sugar and general goods, and get paid for the deliveries each way. Her business must have given her independence, as she didn't marry and have children.

Sometimes Tomas' mother would go with her auntie. They would be away for as long as three weeks, to Hownam or Buchtrig on the Scottish side, or between Uswayford, Ewartly Shank and the Breamish Valley on the English side. Tomas' mother told him that one September, coming back from the Scottish side, his mother and her auntie were caught in a freak snowstorm, and she was hanging round the horse's neck, to keep warm. The hills, the valleys and the rolling grassy tops were thus landscapes which connected people, rather than separated them.

This story is about the drovers, rather than the cattle-stealing reivers, but we can't cross the Cheviot hills without thinking of them. In many ways, the reivers of the fourteenth to seventeenth centuries were the ancestors of the drovers. They rode across the wild hills at night, stealing each other's cattle, burning houses, plundering and raping. They knew the trackways over the hills intimately. "The criminal traffic across the frontier was enormous; it was wild and desolate, and criss-crossed by the secret ways of the raiders, through the mosses and bogs and twisting passes of Cheviot … and the bleak Northumberland valleys."[60]

The knowledge of the hill routes and the skills involved with the driving and management of cattle was passed down from generation to generation, into more peaceful times after the Union of the Crowns in 1603. Cattle stealing was evolving into cattle droving.

A rare picture showing the effect of reiving on women, children and old people.

From Edmund Bogg, 1898

[59] A R B Haldane, p 237
[60] George McDonald Fraser, p 56

Following the Kelso to Morpeth road

It is July 2011, and Mary and I are poised to follow the road again, from Kelso all the way to Morpeth.

It is easy to get to the start of our journey. We'd put our folding bikes on the early morning train from Morpeth to Berwick, and then taken the connecting bus to Kelso. By 10.15, we are in Kelso, ready to start.

George Robson gives a little detail about droving along this route. Yetholm is seven miles south of Kelso:

> Our way from Yetholm was by Cocklawfoot over the Cocklaw or west end of Cheviot, by Uswayford, Wholehope and Alwinton, and thence by Rothbury or Tosson, over the east end of dark Simonside to Longhorsley. This route was chosen because there were no turnpike gates that way between Morpeth and Kelso.

The distance is about fifty miles, probably taking the drovers five or six days.

Kelso to Kale Water

The drovers would pass through the cobbled market place in Kelso, by the ruined abbey, and across the River Tweed. They followed minor roads or tracks leading south over the ridge of hills between the Tweed and the Kale/Bowmont valleys, towards Yetholm. It is a slow steep route for Mary and me, pushing our bikes, through what would have been a landscape of enclosed fields for the drovers, separated by hedged and walled lanes. The wayside flowers are at their best, this July day, colourful with white campion, purple thistles, golden ragwort and blue harebells.

On the top of the ridge is an Ordnance Survey pillar showing 164 metres. Onwards from here are views of the rounded hills of the Scottish side of the Cheviots, big, green, strong and formidable. We can see the valley of the Bowmont Water, at the end of which lies Cocklawfoot farm, and the 15 miles to Kelso milestone.

Near Morebattle Tofts, we meet a farmer, Paul Tinker. He is attending the brown cattle in his field. I ask him if they were shorthorns, the kind which George Robson said were mainly lifted on his droves, and the cattle we see on the old market pictures in Morpeth. He tells me that they were, and that they are having a revival:

> There is a change back to them. Eating trends are changing, and the meat of the shorthorns is popular again. People used to want lean meat with fat round the outside, and this was provided by the European breeds, like the Charollais and the Simmental. Now people want marbled meat like that from the beef shorthorns. The fat is what gives the better flavour.

> It is a matter of finances as well as taste. The shorthorns are more economic these days. The European breeds need to be finished with corn, and this is expensive with the current high price of wheat. The animals have to be kept indoors and fed for the last six months, whereas shorthorns can be finished on grass.

He is an experienced cattle man. This is a good opportunity to keep asking questions. I tell him that Mary and I are following drove roads, and ask if he had ever driven cattle:

> Yes, but only between the two farms we have here, along the minor road, because we don't have cattle handling equipment at one of the farms. It takes an hour at most. We don't have any problem with traffic. This is a rural area and people understand. When I lived in the south, and had dairy cattle, people were in a rush to get to work, and they got annoyed. They don't understand that cows have their pace and can't be rushed.

> There would always have been known tracks, and there would be no ranging over open moorland, with bogs, valley sides and other difficulties to be constantly negotiated. The drovers

would follow tracks with wide verges, and take their time. The cattle can get through boggy land, but it slows them down. They don't like it.

The drovers would always want the shortest way between two points. It's all about selling weight. The further the cattle go in one day, the more they lose weight, because they are not grazing sufficient to maintain their weight. It's like in the western films. They travelled hundreds of miles, needing regular stops and a routine. The drovers would certainly know how far they were going each day, and where the stopping points would be.

The hamlet of Linton, with its prettily sited hilltop church, is near the Kale Water. There are damp fertile fields after the descent, on the river plain, where Morebattle Tofts is sited. This area looks like a suitable overnight or midday stance for drovers.

Kale Water to Cocklawfoot

The B 6401 road between Morebattle and Yetholm runs from west to east here. There is a little ridge between the towns, so that the Kale Water runs to the west, and the Bowmont Water to the north east (NT 800255).   Although they run in different directions, the rivers both eventually arrive at the Tweed, the Kale via the Teviot, and the Bowmont via the Till.

Near here is a sign to Crookedshaws farm, with an old lane marked on the map. We decide to follow this high track. We push up, between stone walls, among the long grass and the flowers, knowing that the drovers came this way. We cross the long distance footpath, St Cuthbert's Way, as it comes down from Crookedshaws hill. Once in the valley of Bowmont Water, cycling is relatively easy.

We are looking again for the milestone which started this whole project in motion. Since last year, we've learned from Iain Davidson that there are several along this road.

Kelso 10 C 5	NT 812244
Kelso 11 C 4	NT 812228
Kelso 13 C 2	NT 821204
Kelso 15 Harbottle 11½	NT 849191

We only find two of them, one by a bridge just past Mowhaugh Farm. It says Kelso 13 and Cocklawfoot 2. Two miles further on, we find the original one, Kelso 15. There it is in its bank, among the buttercups and daisies and the green grass. At the time, we couldn't see the illusive 11½ to Harbottle, as that side of the milestone was still stuck in the bank.

This old RAC sign in the Bowmont valley is warning Mary against sheep!

The Bowmont valley is lined with prehistoric sites. The 1:50,000 and 1: 25,000 Ordnance Survey maps show hilltop forts, cultivation terraces, settlements, homestead and cairns.

There is a leaflet in the series of the South of Scotland Countryside Trails, now out-of-print, which has this to say about the road we are following:

> The farm steading at the end of the quiet public road which winds its way up the sleepy valley of the River Bowmont is now called Cocklawfoot. This is reputed to be the place known in medieval times as 'Hexpathgate', where the wardens of the Middle Marches met during the 15th and 16th centuries to administer law and order … For many years after that, Cocklawfoot was an inn, thriving on the trade of passing drovers. From here, a grassy track climbs steadily upwards through enclosed in-bye fields to open hill. Look out for the old forts above and below the track beyond the shelterbelt.

There is a ford and good access to the streams at Cocklawfoot farm on riverside haughs. It is certainly an ideal place for an overnight stance for the drovers, before tackling the winding, steep, uphill road to the border.

And it is high time for Mary and me to get out the camping stove, the oatmeal and the whisky bottle, while we decide whether or not to attempt the crossing, at 4 o'clock in the afternoon.

Cocklawfoot to Usway Burn
Thousands of cattle walked their way over the border from Scotland to England in the eighteenth and first half of the nineteenth century, and yet there is so little physical evidence of their passing. Here in the Cheviots, among the toll-free border crossings, surely there must be some physical signs of this traffic, rather than simply finding clues from maps and literature, and the fading memories of old people of stories told to them by their grandparents.

This brings us to the word *holloways.*

I'm telling Mary again about the first time I'd heard the word, when I was on an archaeological walk, and the leader used the word to indicate hollowed out pathways where cattle had been driven. Since then, looking out for *holloways,* or hollow ways, is what I do when out on likely drove roads.

And now Mary and I, having decided to go further, are following the drove road up towards the border. What a wonderful, winding green track it is, stretching ahead of us. But the weather is grey and ominous this particular day, and we will have to make camp soon. Then we see them - distinctive holloways made by the cattle, as they were driven up the steep slopes of Outer Cocklaw, approaching the border (NT 868166).

Holloways on the Scottish side of the border, on Clennell Street

Photo: Mary Harris

The South of Scotland Cheviot Routes leaflet says this:

> The clear lines around the hillside at Outer Cocklawfoot could easily be mistaken for the defences of earlier forts, but in fact these mark the former line of the track, which has moved time and again to avoid erosion.

The slope is so steep that we try the twenty-steps-take-a-breath method of pushing our loaded bikes up to the Border.

Pushing south towards the border fence, on Clennell Street

Once past the border fence in England, the path is showing considerable erosion, and we have to go carefully with the bikes. The Cheviot summit is over our left shoulder, with rounded hills rolling away in front and to the west. Soon we are on rough hill grassland, where the cattle could graze, but there is another hour's walking time and another few miles to go until the cattle could reach a good watering place. We go down past Hazely Law to the Usway Burn, where there is a ford and suitable resting place for drovers and cattle beside the burn. It is eight at night, now, and Mary and I put up the tents.

Usway Burn to Alwinton
July it may be, but frost is not far away, at this altitude of 350 metres. We both have four-season sleeping bags, but in the morning Mary tells me that she has hardly slept, and is seriously hypothermic. We agree that we'll have to tuck her up in a heated warm room the next night. Later we learned that the temperature had dropped almost to zero that night. If a storm had come, with gale force winds, we could have died.

Walter Scott recounts a story about the ability of the Highlanders to sleep out in the freezing cold with their cattle. An informant told him that when he had been a young man, he was with a small group of Highlanders and Lowlanders, under the direction of Rob Roy. They had successfully retrieved some stolen cattle. Night had fallen, and the group were set to watch over the cattle:

> The Highlanders, sheltered by their plaids, lay down in the heath comfortably enough, but the Lowlanders had no protection whatsoever. Rob Roy, observing this, directed one of his followers to afford the old man a portion of his plaid, 'for the boy, he may keep himself warm by walking about and watching the cattle'. But as the frost and wind grew more and more cutting, it seemed to freeze the very blood in his young veins. The boy had been exposed to weather all his life, but never could forget the cold of that night; he cursed the bright moon for giving no heat with so much light.

At length, the sense of cold and weariness became so intolerable, that ... he couched himself down beside one of the most bulky of the Highlanders ... he coveted a share of his plaid, and by imperceptible degrees drew a corner of it round him. He was now comparatively in paradise, and slept sound until daybreak.   When he awoke, he was terribly afraid on observing that his nocturnal operations had altogether uncovered the Highlander's neck and shoulders ... which were covered with hoar frost. However, the man got up and shook himself, rubbing off the hoar frost with his plaid, and muttering something of a *cauld neight*, they then drove on the cattle without further adventure.[61]

Our day's way now leads diagonally up another green path, with short sheep-grazed turf, and the sound of the waterfall in the Usway Burn as it tumbles over the volcanic rocks into a turf-brown pool. It is a particularly pretty part of the journey.

Soil reversal improves the paths

Credit for this attractive part of Clennell Street leading up from the Usway Burn towards Kidland Forest, (NT 876137 to 879128), must go to volunteers from the British Horse Society, working together on both sides of the Border.

They encouraged Northumberland National Park and the Tweed Trails Trust staff to improve the path after first becoming aware of a new technique being used on the Southern Upland Way. Known as soil reversal, which includes essential drainage work, it has turned impassable boggy sections into well drained stone-based tracks which have grassed over in a couple of years. It is so successful that hardly anyone travelling on them now would be able to identify which bits were repaired in the 1990s.   This technique was developed in the 1980s by a Scottish contractor to improve the surface of the West Highland Way, a long distance walking route that was very boggy.

Sometimes, we just enjoy our wild places without realising the hard work that has made it possible.

Photo: W P Collier, taken shortly before 1914.

---

[61] Walter Scott, *Rob Roy,* pp 444 - 445

Reproduced with permission of Bellingham Heritage Centre and S F Owen

The path leads now through forestry, with some deeply rutted places and large areas of felling. It is not the most charming part of Clennell Street. We move on as far as the remains of Wholehope Cottage. A shepherd's dwelling was there during drover times. Wholehope's earliest recorded date is 1233, when it was part of the upland estate of the monks at Newminster Abbey.[62] The cottage was photographed in the early decades of the twentieth century by the Bellingham photographer W P Collier.[63]

It was farmed until the 1940s, when it became a youth hostel. My sister and I stayed there in 1962, when the water supply was an enamel can which you left out all night under a trickle of water, to catch the drips. In the morning, the water in the can was full of little black leaches. The building is now demolished. There is nothing more there than the outline of the walls, and a corrugated iron sheep handling shed (NT 901093).

The next couple of miles south towards Alwinton contain many prehistoric sites. This route has been walked by the feet of humans and their animals, for thousands of years. Here are cairns, field systems of probably Bronze Age date, roundhouses of Iron Age/Roman date, and much more. Mary and I had copies of Northumberland County Council's Historic Environment Record for many of these sites, and we enjoyed ourselves trying to locate some of them, and playing with my new GPS. We settled ourselves on the former palisaded settlement of Hoseden Linn, and gazed ahead as the drovers would have done, at the ridges of the Simonside hills, lying ahead to the south. This would be the next day's work, crossing them on the way to Morpeth.

There are several cross-ridge dykes across Clennell Street here, and they are not too hard to spot. One is just south of Hoseden Linn, at NT 918081. They are earthen banks and ditches, cutting across the track at right angles. There are different interpretations of what they are, including the possibility that they were used by drovers in the past. An archaeologist Paul Frodsham writes:

> These cross ridge dykes are undated, but may well date originally from later prehistory. Their original form is also unknown: they may have been crowned with a timber palisade. Their function must have been to help to control movement of people and livestock along the line of Clennell Street ... who would have had to pass through narrow gaps in these dykes which presumably would have been gated.[64]

The cross-ridge dyke just south of Hoseden Linn on Clennell Street. It runs across the centre of the picture. NT 918081

[62] Richard Carlton, Appendix 1 Clennell Street, site 35
[63] S F Owen, p 30
[64] Paul Frodsham, pp 135 - 136

We are now descending to Alwinton, and after the chilly wind blowing along the tops, it is like coming down into a land of civilisation. Here are cottages with blue delphiniums and orange marigolds in the gardens, and roses clambering up the walls. In the garden of the Rose and Thistle, visitors are enjoying the weather, children playing with a Jack Russell puppy, and apples ripening on the trees. The drovers too would have enjoyed the hospitality, resting their cattle or sheep on farmland nearby. For them, it would be a well earned respite, after the passage along Clennell Street, and the arrival into England. As for us, we received rather a quizzical glance when we asked the host at the inn for a heated bedroom for the night. He looked at our folding bikes, and said: "You didn't come over Clennell Street with those, did you?"

Alwinton to Forestburn Gate
One and a half more days' droving would have brought the animals to Morpeth now. For the drovers, it wouldn't be as difficult as the day before, but even so, the Simonside range had to be crossed or worked round.

There were several ways for the drovers to get from Alwinton to Morpeth. They could head for Rothbury, but it is worth noting that as recently as Armstrong's map of 1769, there was no road from there to Weldon Bridge. Thus if they were leaving Rothbury for Morpeth as recently as the late eighteenth century, they would have had to use what are now back roads via either Netherwitton or Todburn.

Mary and I decide to follow the road towards Tosson, one of the ways mentioned by George Robson. We cycle through Harbottle and Holystone, both villages with inns which were used by drovers according to local tradition. The meanders of the River Coquet enclose wide grassy haughlands, places where cattle could be watered or rested.

We pass Woodhouses Bastle, the fortified farmhouse near Holystone, which was inhabited until the early twentieth century. It would have been an ordinary dwelling house for country people, if cold and comfortless, in the days of the drovers.

Chirnside bastle, a tall narrow building not unlike Woodside. Cattle were housed in the lower part of these fortified farmhouses, the family living above.

From Hodgson, 1835

There was an inn at tiny Swindon, at the junction on the road between Rothbury and Elsdon. David Dippie Dixon tells us that it was called The Badger.[65]

There is a droving road over Whitefield Hill to Chartners which leads from near here. It slopes away steeply uphill to the south west, then to the south east. It passes a standing stone on Darden Rigg which was still there in 1806,[66] and was probably used as a landmark to keep travellers on the track. This bridle way is now for access during grouse management. It goes through Harwood Forest and out past Fallowlees cottage, from where the drovers would make their way to Morpeth or Newcastle.

We head for Tosson, passing the farms which lie along the foot of the Simonside range. Here too was a public house in the 1800s called the Royal George.[67]

(There is an exhilarating alternative route that drovers took from Tosson. This is called the Cambo Bridle Road. It is for walkers only and it has its own short chapter following this.)

We push our bicycles past Tosson, up the steep hill towards the forestry car park, and along the upland road by Lordenshaws hillfort. As we crest the hill, we realise that the road itself is laid in one of several holloways formed by the cattle in whose tracks we are following. We can see their corrugated outline on the skyline ahead of us (NZ 046991).

Lordenshaws hill fort is on our left. Walkers and visitors are exploring it, and others are climbing up the path to Dove Crag and Simonside on our right.

We go on down the hill, past ancient woodland with alder and hazel, heading for the Forestburn Gate pub. The route briefly coincides with the 1751 turnpike road between Hexham and Alnmouth, now the B 6342. The name of the pub is another reminder that a toll gate and smithy were once sited here.

Forestburn Gate to Morpeth

Drovers could slake their thirst at the Crown and Thistle, as the Forestburn Gate was formerly called. The back road is signed to Morpeth from here. We join the network of lanes among which we approached Morpeth on the Coldstream route. The drovers would need to avoid their animals getting into the fields sown with arable crops, or mingling with sheep or cattle of the local farmers, along these lanes. They probably would send one of the lads on ahead to ensure that all the gates were closed, or use their clever dogs.

As they came within a mile or two of Morpeth, they would be likely to meet other drovers with their animals. They would be coming from Wingates, from Netherwitton and Pigdon, from Hartburn and Throphill, and from Meldon and Mitford. On the days before and after the market, there must have been opportunities for farmers to their rent fields for overnight stances along the way.

From Netherwitton, Mary and I reach West Benridge, and decide to follow a quiet bridleway which is called Dark Lane on the first edition 1860s Ordnance Survey map, and a likely route for drovers in the past. It opens out next to a wooded enclosure with spaced out trees giving shelter. There is a reedy depression nearby in the field, which looks as though it may have been managed as a pond for animals. Today, livestock in the fields are watered from old sinks, bathtubs and metal tanks. Rusting farm machinery lies overgrown with weeds in the hedgerows. The corrugations of ridge and furrow in fields where sheep are grazing are signs of a historic landscape, quite different from the hill landscapes the drovers have passed over.

---

[65] David Dippie Dixon, *Upper Coquetdale,* pp 304 and 323
[66] 1806 Tosson or Hepple Enclosure Award and Plan, 1806
[67] David Dippie Dixon, p 323

Leading down Mitford Dean to the River Font is one of the most classic of holloways. The steep-sided track is known as Clarty Lonnen, and muddy it certainly is. Once at the River Font there are several old fords, one still in regular use. The grassy haughs in the meandering curves of the river look like perfect overnight stances for droves of animals.

Clarty Lonnen

From Mitford, it is only just over a mile to Morpeth. As we cycle under the A1 bypass, we are reminded how the times have changed. Following the centuries of walking slowly to the markets, over the hills and along the lanes, the cattle and sheep are now driven to their final destination in motor wagons along the dual carriageway.

Herds of shaggy cattle, driven by their whiskery drovers, over the secretive mosses and
moorlands of Simonside; shelters under rocky overhangs; packhorse trails and whisky
smuggling; hideouts for Covenanters and mosstroopers; the forgotten Cambo Bridle Road
reveals all these secrets.

I had found a brief mention of it in the book *Archaeology in Northumberland National Park*, in a
chapter called *Simonside: From prehistory to present*.   What was this evocatively named
route? Following the references led me to the Northumberland National Park report,
Simonside Archaeological Landscape Study.   The next thing was a visit to Woodhorn to see
the 1806 Tosson Common enclosure award, where the road is labelled faintly on the plan.
The enclosure award names the township of Tosson as being responsible for the upkeep of
the Cambo Bridle Road to the width of 6 feet, and describes its route:

> It begins at the south end of Great Tosson Lane and leading from thence Westward to the west
> side of the little Hill and from thence southward by the west side of Simonside to Browns Cross
> where the said bridle road enters the ancient lands of Spylaw belong to his grace the Duke of
> Northumberland.[68]

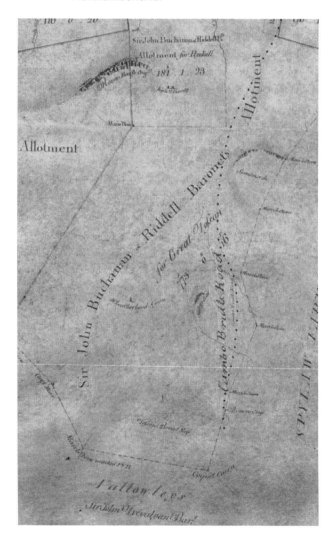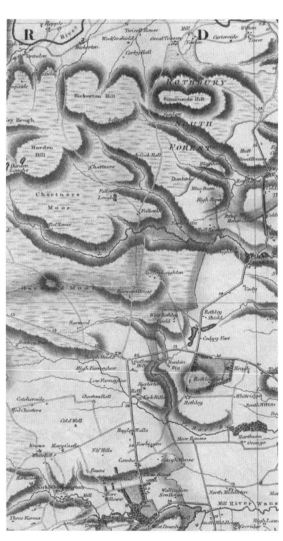

Left above: an extract from the Tosson or Hepple Enclosure Plan, annotated to highlight the route of the
Cambo Bridle Road.
Map: reproduced with permission of Northumberland Archives

---

[68] Tosson or Hepple Enclosure Plan and Award, 1806 – 1807

Right above: The Fryer map of 1820 shows the road heading south from Great Tosson, between Simonside and Bickerton Hill. It also shows the track to the west of Bickerton Hill, through Chartners. This is the one over Whitefield Hill, described earlier. Both meet at Fallowlees.
Map reproduced with permission of Northumberland Archives

Drovers following the Cambo Bridle Road would pass between Simonside and Ravensheugh, cross the heathery bogs to the south, and arrive at Cambo via Fallowlees and Greenleighton on the Wallington estate lands. From there, they would make their way onwards easterly to Morpeth market, or south towards Newcastle.

The Cambo Bridle Road was an important thoroughfare in its time, used by drovers and pack horse teams. In modern times, it has survived as a line of footpaths and bridleways. The last stretch to Cambo is along minor roads.

Adventurous walkers can follow it as a linear walk all the way from Great Tosson to Cambo, a distance of 10 miles. Or it can be done in two halves, returning the same way each time. Much of the southern half is cyclable, with good planning. In August 2011, I followed the northern half in the company of Iain Hedley, one of the authors of the Simonside study, and archaeologist, Ian Colquhoun who had introduced me to holloways.

Great Tosson to Selby's Cove
The Cambo Bridle Road heads south from Tosson Burgh, the single-walled hill fort where the Iron Age people could look north over the Coquet Valley as far as the rounded outline of the Cheviots (NU 023005). There are holloways winding around the hill fort, and the tracks pass the watering point of Slatebrae Well, with its overhanging mountain ash. The green road leads towards the forest, with views of the enclosed fields to the west, over the valley of the little Chesterhope Burn. All of landscape history seems to be here, including the presence of long gone British wild animals in the farm name of Wolfershiel, just a little further west.

Slatebrae Well, at Tosson Burgh

David Dippie Dixon includes many tales about this area in his 1903 book *Upper Coquetdale*.[69] At Wolfershiel, he tells us that in 1836 the farmer and tenant were heavily fined after being caught by mounted excisemen for illicit whisky distilling.

---

[69] David Dippie Dixon, pp 322 – 325 and pp 486 - 489

In the forest, the footpath marked with yellow arrows follows the old bridle road, past a distinctive rock overhang, which may have been used as a refuge in times long gone. Before the days of forestry, it would have had wide views over the Coquet Valley (NU022991).

Soon afterwards, the path leads over a large flat sandstone outcrop, which has been cut into criss-cross patterns by unknown drivers of animals. This must be one of the most charming and original marked rocks in Northumberland. A friend who is an expert on pack-horse roads says she has never seen such a thing before.

> The boulder appears to have a carved surface forming a 'cobbled' pattern, presumably in order to facilitate grip for packhorse and livestock. The eastern edge is considerably worn, which may have been caused by cart wheels. A little further on is a similar but smaller stone situated in the base of a holloway. It consists of horizontal lines c 0.70m apart carved at right angles to the path (NZ 023991 and 022989).[70]

Criss-cross marked stone, believed to have been cut to stop the feet of pack horses from slipping

Further on, as the path opens out from the forest into the heather moorland, the multiple paths typical of cattle movements appear.

> A series of at least 29 distinct hollow ways run along the western side of Spital Hill, crossing the col between Simonside Hill and Ravensheugh and continuing southwards … They are generally steep sided with rounded bottoms. They are likely to represent the 'sheep walks' mentioned by Dixon.[71]

There is an easily identifiable Bronze Age cairn beside the path between Simonside and Ravensheugh (NZ 020987).

> Despite considerable disturbance from forestry and earlier excavation, it retains a domed appearance…Several hollow ways lead up towards the cairn and it may have been used in later periods as a way marker.[72]

From here, walkers and climbers can reach both peaks to the west and east, but the Cambo Bridle Path keeps going south, along the heathery, boggy track towards the Ousen House.

[70] Lancaster University Archaeological Unit, p 80
[71]   "   "   "   p 76
[72]   "   "   "   p 76

What on earth is this strangely named Ousen House? I'd been unable to imagine this moorland refuge, but find it to be a craggy outcrop, long and low (NZ 023980). Under the rocky overhang is a large room-like space, with what had been a fireplace and an opening to the sky at the back. This is where drovers could shelter for the night. Heathery moorland and evidence of holloways stretch away to the east and the south, the way the drovers were heading.

The Ousen House, a possible overnight stopping place for drovers

It is still an appealing camping place, and there are traces of modern seekers of solitude in the ashes of a camp fire with rusty cans and plastic rubbish. This won't be left for future archaeologists, as Iain Hedley says he'll get the National Park wardens to clear it up.

Dippie Dixon mentioned the Ousen house. "Underneath its shelving rock cattle may have sheltered".[73] As for its name, it could be based on old words from the Welsh *iesin* meaning 'fine, fair, beautiful, handsome; radiant, sparkling, shimmering, bright, gleaming'.[74] However I prefer a different interpretation, the lowland Scots word *ousen* or *owsen,* as another word for *oxen.*[75]

The landscape south from here dips gradually over heather, bog and upland pasture in the parts where it is not forested. Selby's Cove is a big cut in the land, a little ahead of the Ousen House. Dippie Dixon called it "a rocky defile on the south side of the hill, in which, tradition says, a Coquetdale mosstrooper named Selby had his retreat in the old border days. It is now a famous refuge for foxes".[76]

Selby's Cove to Cambo
Crossing the boggy heathery mosses between Selby's Cove and the start of the forest towards Fallowlees would be dangerous if it were not for the National Park staff, who have created boardwalks over the worst parts. Near here are the lichen covered remains of the walls of an isolated shepherd's cottage (NZ 021975). It was already in ruins at the time of the first edition 1860s Ordnance Survey map. Yet drovers must have passed by, and exchanged news with the people they found there.

[73] David Dippie Dixon, Upper Coquetdale, p 482
[74] Lancaster University Archaeological Unit, p 15
[75] *Dictionary of the Scots Language*, www.dsl.ac.uk, search under "ox"
[76] David Dippie Dixon, Upper Coquetdale, p 483

Left: ruined remains of a shepherd's cottage near Selby's Cove

Below: shepherd James Tait, in his cottage in the Yarrow valley, Scottish borders, 1898
From Edmund Bogg

This is a true wilderness area, with scarcely any hedges or walls. Much of it is Open Access Land, and marked as such on modern maps. The drovers and pack horse men who crossed it over the centuries must have followed known paths where the animals could pass without danger of being caught in the morass.

The dangers of the peat bogs

Hughie Mather is a former forestry worker, who now lives in Harwood village, not far from Fallowlees. He is an octogenarian, and still cycles regularly on his mountain bike all over the tracks in this area at the back of Simonside. He knows about the bogs.

"There was this hired machine, which used to pull tree stumps out of the ground. The stumps went into a funnel, and came out chipped. It was a massive machine.

"In this particular place the peat was 35 feet deep, and it was soft and shaky. We had to lay the remains of the trees over it to make a pathway. The machine travelled along it all right, but then it began to creep off the pathway. It started to sink. It just went down gradually. The driver leapt off. He wouldn't be staying on, now would he? In the end only the exhaust funnel was sticking out.

"The environmental people wanted the machine out. We got two tractors to pull it, but they very nearly went in too. And it is still there!

"Once we were erecting a deer fence round some newly planted trees. We'd done it scores of times. We used a county tractor with a post knocker, which was controlled inside the cab with a lever, and it pounded in the post. Philip was controlling and I was holding the post. I shouted to Philip as usual, and he gave it a couple of knocks, and swoosh – no post. It was 9 feet long, and it just disappeared.

"The drovers would have known the bad places, and where they shouldn't go. This area is 70% peat. Normally it is 4 foot deep, but in certain parts it is down to 35 feet. If cattle go to drink in the pools, their front legs sink in, and there is no way of getting them out. I've seen a horse go down when it was leading trees. We got it out, but with difficulty."

Once in the forest, there are the overgrown remains of a former hunting lodge, known as Black Cock Hall (NZ 021962). This is shown on maps of 1820, 1828 and 1860, but by the latest date it is marked as a ruin. The new long distance footpath, St Oswald's Way, follows the former Cambo Bridle Road through the forest some of the time now, to Fallowlees farmhouse (NZ 019943).

Dippie Dixon has more old stories to tell us:

> At Fallowlees, amid the wilds of Simonside, William Veitch, a leader of the Scotch Covenanters, found a safe refuge where he lived for several years. After his flight from Pentland fight in 1666, he continued to preach in various parts of Redesdale, Coquetdale and the borders thereabout." In 1671, "he removed his wife and two sons, William and Samuel, in creels from Edinburgh into a village called Falalies.[77]

At Fallowlees are the ruined walls of a bastle, one of Northumberland's fortified farmhouses dating back to the unsettled days of the reivers. This is the building likely to have sheltered William Veitch.

From Fallowlees, the spreading open slopes to Greenleighton farm lie up to the southern skyline. The drovers and their animals caused more holloways to be formed on the south bank of the Fallowlees Burn as they made their way onward.

A little further ahead is one of the prettiest green roads that I ever saw. It runs along a raised surface, above the level of the brownish reedy upland pasture. Originally, it was bounded by big stones, some still prominent, but many half buried in the banks. There is a ford with big flagstones over a tiny moorland stream. This made-up road may have been part of landscape improvements in the mid 1700s, which would impede the free movement of the drovers.

The path between Fallowlees and Greenleighton. It is not marked on all maps, but is open to walkers on Access Land.

Sir Walter Blackett - no friend to the drovers
In 1727, Sir Walter Blackett inherited the Wallington estate from his uncle, Sir William Blackett. His twentieth century successor, Sir Charles Trevelyan, tells us what the land was like at the time:

> When Sir Walter Blackett took over his uncle's estate at Wallington, it was largely a conglomeration of ragged, unfenced crofts and pastures, and undrained fells and moors. In 1728, there were no enclosures except rude earth banks which could be climbed by cattle or

---

[77] David Dippie Dixon, Upper Coquetdale, p 487

leapt by sheep; no roads other than horse-tracks or, at best, cart-tracks winding in and out through the fields from farm to farm.

Sir Walter left it a noble and well-ordered property. He constructed and maintained very many miles of excellent roads ready for stage coaches when they should make their appearance, and running straight over such long tracts of country that a stranger to the district is apt to enquire whether he is driving on an ancient roman highway. He built or restored his farmsteads and outlying cottages. It was then probably that the pele towers disappeared from the countryside, though the farms remain on the same sites, generally on the tops of the ridges from which raiders could be sighted coming from the north.[78]

An estate plan commissioned by Sir William Blackett was produced in 1728. It gives us some clues about the open, unfenced landscape before the enclosures, and shows the "cart tracks winding in and out through the fields from farm to farm". A track coming towards Fallowlees from the north west would have led from Whitefield past Chartners, a route shown on the Fryer's map earlier in this chapter. The Cambo Bridle Road isn't shown.

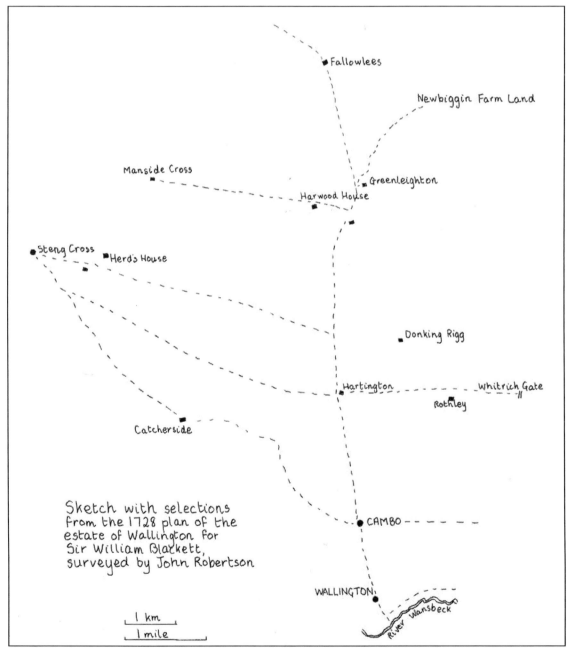

[78] Sir Charles Trevelyan, pp 17 - 18

From Hartington an intriguing path is shown running just north of Rothley to the boundary of the estate, at a point marked as Whitrich Gate, in the general direction of Morpeth. Whitridge, as it is now spelled, is a farm between Rothley and Longwitton (NZ 061882). There is indeed an old-fashioned gate here, which causes me to wonder if it was used in an early attempt to control the movement of drovers and their animals.

Before 1728, those earthen banks described by Sir Charles Trevelyan, which could easily be climbed by cattle or leapt by sheep, were not much of an obstruction to the drovers. By the time of the next Wallington survey plan in 1742, the fields near the Hall have much squarer edges and tree emblems appear along their boundaries. Drovers are beginning to be obliged to use the roads.

By the time of the third Wallington plan of 1777, a clear straight road is shown for the first time which is the new road between Morpeth and Elsdon. We'll meet this turnpike in a later chapter.

The Cambo Bridle Road may have been coming towards the end of its useful life as the roads improved under the guidance of landowners like Sir Walter Blackett, but it was still of sufficient importance to feature in the 1806 enclosure award, and on Fryer's and Greenwood's maps of 1820 and 1828. As we have seen, it can still be followed, if care is taken. Like so many of these ancient droving tracks, it owes its present-day survival to the efforts of people who ensured that they were legally safeguarded. Without their work, ancient tracks like the forgotten Cambo Bridle Road could be lost for ever.

The new live hedges

Bailey and Culley describe the "new mode of raising fences". They write that Walter Trevelyan Esq of Netherwitton erected an earth mound, seven feet wide at the bottom and five feet high, on the top of which he planted a row of quicks, probably hawthorn, and on each side willow stakes which take root and form a live fence. The authors also describe stone walls used for fences, the usual dimension being two and a half feet at the bottom, and about four feet high. The expense of the earth fences was two shillings and sixpence for every seven yards, and about six shillings for the stone walls. It took twelve or more cartloads to create seven yards of stone wall. They state that "the advantages of enclosing private property" mean that the proprietor can separate land of different qualities, thus better managing it, and he can control the "whims of the shepherd and the teazings of his dog".

Bailey and Culley,1805, pp 60 - 62

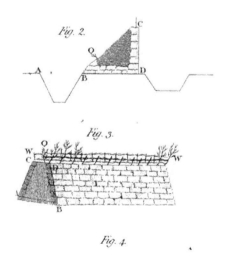

COUNTY SURVEYOR'S OFFICE

SURVEYS AND MAPS
of
PUBLIC RIGHTS OF WAY

for the purposes of PART IV of the
National Parks and Access to the
Countryside Act, 1949

Memorandum prepared by the COMMONS,
OPEN SPACES AND FOOTPATHS
PRESERVATION SOCIETY in collabo-
ration with the Ramblers Association;
recommended by the County Councils
Association

and approved by the
MINISTRY OF TOWN AND COUNTRY PLANNING

COMMONS, OPEN SPACES AND FOOTPATHS
PRESERVATION SOCIETY
71 ECCLESTON SQUARE, WESTMINSTER, S.W.1

January, 1950   Price 9d.

*The little green booklet
which advised councils on
how to implement rights of
way legislation, still at
County Hall in Morpeth*

THE TIMES
TUESDAY SEPTEMBER 20 1960

Home News

ARMY SEEK TO CLOSE PATHS

COURT TOLD OF USE IN 16TH CENTURY

FROM OUR SPECIAL CORRESPONDENT
ROTHBURY, Sept. 19

SHEPHERDS ON NARROW PATHS

MEMORIES OF FORMER USAGE

FROM OUR SPECIAL CORRESPONDENT
ROTHBURY, Sept. 20

SETTLEMENT AT PATH INQUIRY

LIBERTY FOR PUBLIC "SUBSTANTIAL"

FROM OUR SPECIAL CORRESPONDENT
ROTHBURY, Sept. 21

THE JOURNAL THURSDAY SEPTEMBER 22 1960

PARTIES AGREE ON BORDER RIGHTS OF WAY

AN appeal committee of Northumberland Quarter Sessions, sitting at Rothbury, closed its hearing of a dispute involving 93 footpaths and bridal paths in the Cheviots when it was announced that the two parties concerned had reached an agreement.

The Times
September 30 1960

GAIN FOR COUNTRY LOVERS

MANY RIGHTS OF WAY OVER RANGE PRESERVED

FROM OUR CORRESPONDENT
NEWCASTLE UPON TYNE, Sept. 29

*Cuttings from The Times and The Journal about the final days of
the saving of paths in the Otterburn Ranges
Reproduced with thanks to Julian Philipson*

The freedom to drive their animals over the moors and hills, without obstruction, was essential to the drovers. In the enclosed lowland landscapes, they needed the right to pass along traditional paths and roads, between the stone walls and hedgerows. It was an economic necessity, but it was something more. As their freedoms were curtailed, they had to pay to use turnpikes along roads that they had used for generations, and they certainly resented it.

To this day, we feel that the country we live in belongs to us. We should be able to move freely around, because we always have; because our ancestors did, right back through history. And the remarkable fact is that we can. The rights of the drovers to use the ancient roads across the Cheviots, and along the local tracks towards the markets such as Morpeth's, have become enshrined in law as everybody's rights.

These are our rights of way. They are of inestimable value. They give us the freedom of the countryside. We can walk on them, ride horses or bicycles along the bridleways, and the landowners have an obligation to keep the access open, providing gates and stiles as necessary. Thus, we don't have to be owners of the countryside to be able to enjoy it. With maps in our hand, we can plan routes wherever we choose. We can walk from Morpeth to Greenock, like the woman who was doing just that along Rimside Moor in the nineteenth century. We can walk over private land, along the rights of way, wherever they exist.

The saving of the drove roads and all the other rights of way, is a remarkable story. How is it that we can follow our inclination, and walk or ride along this network that covers the country? We can't necessarily do it in other countries. In Scotland, with generally excellent access provision, rights of way aren't marked as such on the maps, and a path which is on the map does not necessarily exist in practice. Neither can the authorities always enforce it to be maintained so that it can be used.

In Ireland, coastal paths marked on the map can be blocked off with locked gates and barbed wire. In the United States, paths exist in national parks, but in the ordinary open countryside, you are risking your life trying to take a walk across private land, such is the national obsession with private property.

In France, there are the wonderful Grandes Randonnées, but other little tracks which might appear on the maps are not necessarily there in practice. I admit that I am generalising from my own experience, only knowing the countries through which I've personally adventured. Also, I am differentiating between two kinds of paths. The marked long distance footpaths are created especially to encourage walkers to enjoy the countryside in a safely constricted way. Then there are the ordinary everyday routes which country people took in the past, to the local church, from farm to farm, to the village or the market, to the road where the country bus could be picked up.

This chapter is an attempt to give credit to those who saved our drove roads, and all the other traditional routes that our ancestors walked before us. It is a national achievement. In Northumberland, as everywhere in the country, we have had people who have dedicated their time to safeguarding these freedoms. Yet, they are seldom hailed. Who knows about them? When did it happen? Is it still going on? How could I find out?

I took as my starting point the National Parks and Countryside Act of 1949, set up by the new post-war Labour government. It gave the duty to all county councils in England and Wales to survey and put on a map all the public rights of way in existence at that time. The procedure had three mapping stages: draft, provisional and definitive. By the time any path reached the definitive map, it was legally protected, and it would stay that way, even if it was little or never used in the future.

It was an amazingly complex job. Writers John Riddall and John Trevelyan, who continue to advise on rights of way, put it like this. "Early hopes of a swift completion of the initial task of surveying and preparing maps were not realised as insufficient resources were made available by many councils. The compulsory survey in the counties was finally completed with the publication of the definitive map of North Bedfordshire in May 1982."[79]

Here in Northumberland, it took a mere eleven years, being completed by December 1960. In the 1950s, County Hall was still in Newcastle, near the castle keep. To try to work out how it was done, I tackled the minutes books of Northumberland County Council's Bridges and Roads Committee, who were responsible for footpaths. Working through the neatly bound books at Northumberland Archives in Woodhorn, and using the index, I was able to piece together the procedure. The minutes record only the barebones story, and debate among the councillors on the committee was virtually never recorded. A few local newspaper reports put some colour into the story, although they were hard to find. I still find it difficult to accept that such a fundamentally important story is so little remembered.

In June 1949, the clerk to the county council informed the Bridges and Roads committee of the task that lay ahead.[80]

> The County Council's first duty will be within three years from the passing of the Act, unless the time is extended, to make a survey of all the public paths which include both footpaths and bridleways in their area, and to embody the results in a draft map and statement.
>
> County District and Parish Councils may be called upon for information to help in this task. The draft map has to be advertised, and representations and objections considered, and there is a right of appeal.
>
> A provisional map has next to be prepared and advertised, and at this stage landowners and occupiers may apply to Quarter Sessions for a declaration that the map is incorrect.
>
> Finally, a definitive map is to be prepared and advertised in the *London Gazette*; this map is then conclusive for ordinary purposes as to the existence, position and width of public paths.

The councillors were thus prepared for what was to come. The Bridges and Roads Committee took over responsibility for the procedure, and the staff at County Hall would undertake the work involved.

The map of councils within the county of Northumberland was quite different at this time. There were Municipal Borough Councils - Morpeth, Wallsend, Blyth, Whitley Bay and Berwick; and Urban District Councils - Hexham, Prudhoe, Newburn, Gosforth, Longbenton, Bedlingtonshire, Ashington, Newbiggin, Amble, Alnwick and Seaton Valley. These councils served the towns themselves, rather than the countryside which surrounded them.

There were also ten Rural District Councils, covering large areas of countryside - Morpeth, Haltwhistle, Hexham, Castle Ward (Ponteland), Bellingham, Rothbury, Alnwick, Glendale, Belford and Norham & Islandshire. There were 450 parishes within the Rural Districts. Each parish had to survey its own area, if necessary setting up a special committee to do so. The County Council knew that the process would be much quicker with the Municipal Borough Councils than with the Rural Districts.

The Commons Open Spaces and Footpaths Preservation Society produced a little green briefing booklet called *Surveys and Maps of Public Rights of Way*, and provided it to all the county councils.[81] It has survived in the files at Northumberland's County Hall in Morpeth to this day. Each parish needed a set of the six-inch to the mile Ordnance Survey quarter-sheets covering its territory. The society told the county councils that the maps could be obtained

---

[79] John Riddall and John Trevelyan, p 73
[80] Bridges and Roads Committee Minutes, vol 21, pp 15 – 17
[81] Commons, Open Spaces and Footpaths Preservations Society, p4

from a local bookseller or from Stanfords in London, at two shillings for each copy. As many parishes in Northumberland are so large, it was no trivial expense, but it seems the county council took over this responsibility and the cost.

By September 1952, the county surveyor reported to the Bridges and Roads Committee that during the winter of 1950 and the early part of 1951, the county council staff sent sets of maps, photocopied from the 6" Ordnance Survey, to all the district councils in Northumberland listed above. The Rural District councils then had to disperse them to all the parishes, so they could mark the paths they considered to be rights of way.[82]

The county surveyor doesn't say if the hundreds of maps were delivered by hand, or posted, but in either case it was no small procedure.

Once the parish committees received the maps they had to tackle the enormous job of identifying the footpaths, and the little green booklet instructs them how it was to be done.

First, they had to consult other maps and documents, which include "Inclosure Award maps, Tithe maps, parish maps, maps of admitted public rights of way deposited by owners under Section 1 (4) of the Rights of Way Act of 1932, statements in writing by owners expressly dedicating paths, old Ordnance Surveys, maps in local guide books and histories, footpath rambling guides and old parish council minutes".[83]

That could have been a very interesting job for committee members who liked delving into old documents. Others must have wondered where on earth they would find the time.

The little green book helpfully informs the committee where these documents are to be found, and how to define which paths "must be presumed to have been 'dedicated' as public rights of way because they have been used by the public as of right and without interference for not less than 20 years".

The information, once compiled and understood, should be marked on the maps "in *ordinary* pencil" at first, with a single continuous line for each way and number, or a broken line in cases of doubt. Special care "should be taken to include any paths believed to be public but omitted from the Ordnance Survey". More instructions follow:

> The Committee should now walk over the whole of the reputed public ways in the parish, to confirm that they exist and to note their condition: to ensure that they have not omitted any path, and to enable them to complete the numbering and other marking of the maps.[84]

I had to laugh at this point. That is all very well for younger and fitter members of the committee, who enjoy walking. Let us hope that each committee had such members. As it is often retired people who have the time to serve on committees, and that many of them must not have been as fit as they once were, this could have been another cause for inward groans. But perhaps the general level of fitness was higher in the fifties.

The area was to be surveyed, path by path, and a schedule detailing the exact location of the start and finish of each numbered path was to be made, with details of its condition, existing usage and rights, and with the date and names of who walked it.

The little green book then describes an annual review:

> All public paths should be systematically perambulated once a year, and a report should be presented to the Parish Council upon their condition at each perambulation. It is suggested that

---

[82] Bridges and Roads Committee Minutes, vol 22 p 45
[83] Commons, Open Spaces and Footpaths Preservation Society, pp 4 - 5
[84]   "   "   "   "   "   p 8

Rogation Sunday might be a suitable day for this annual perambulation, as it is already associated with the ancient custom of 'beating the bounds'.[85]

Somehow, I think this suggestion is likely to have been widely ignored!

The booklet concludes that "the first complete survey will constitute a kind of 'Domesday' book of Rights of Way".
Northumberland's Roads and Bridges committee met four times a year, and the county surveyor who had been appointed to supervise the process, always gave a report.

In September 1952, the minutes record him saying:

> Despite a number of attempts to expedite these local surveys, however, up to now the maps and accompanying statements have only been completed by seven authorities, the Borough Councils of Berwick upon Tweed, Morpeth and Wallsend, and the Urban District Councils of Alnwick, Gosforth, Newbiggin and Newburn; the necessary information has thus still to be obtained for one borough and seven urban districts, while in the case of the rural districts completed maps have been received for only 141 parishes out of a total of 451.

Progress was being made on the towns, and they were one third of the way through the rural areas.[86]

By June 1953, 212 out of 450 parishes were returned. Nearly half way now, in the rural areas.

At this meeting, the county surveyor acknowledged the help of the voluntary sector.

> The Ramblers Association are prepared to help with the work of walking the paths, but it will be necessary for the Council's own staff to interview local people to obtain the necessary details about paths claimed as rights of way.[87]

Exactly how much time, how many weekends, how many resources the Ramblers were putting in to this process is not clear from the minutes, but it must have been considerable.

By September 1953, the county surveyor reported that they needed a fourth year, and that the council was applying for an extension to allow the work to go on until December 1954. By this time, 230 out of the 450 parishes in the rural areas had completed the Draft Maps. Getting closer.[88]

In September 1954, the county surveyor reported:

> The draft maps for all the county districts have been submitted to the Committee, and the next stage is the preparation of provisional maps and statements. I recommend the Committee to approve these, to fix the relevant date for this portion of the survey and to give instructions as to the depositing of the maps and statements for inspection, and the publication of notices of the deposit.[89]

By the county districts, he meant the Borough and Urban District Councils for the town, and not the rural areas.

Once the Draft Maps were all deposited, the objectors would get the chance to have their say, and also it provided for further representations to be made on paths which should be added.

---

[85] Commons, Open Spaces and Footpaths Preservation Society, p 14 - 15
[86] Bridges and Roads Committee Minutes, vol 22 p 45
[87]   "   "   "   vol 22 p 135
[88]   "   "   "   vol 22 pp 164 - 165
[89]   "   "   "   vol 22 p 295

Westminster VIPs have tea at Uswayford

The new Labour government of Clement Attlee had promoted the National Park and Countryside Act of 1949, and Members of Parliament were keen to follow the progress of the Rights of Way procedure. It became the practice of a party of Labour Members of Parliament to walk sections of the newly formed Pennine Way each Whit weekend.

In 1950, John Philipson from Harbottle acted as their guide, over a three day walk through the Cheviots. On the second day, they stopped at Uswayford for tea, and to meet the Telfer family. The VIPs included the Minister of Town and Country Planning Hugh Dalton who was also president of the Ramblers' Association, Barbara Castle MP for Blackburn, George Chetwynd MP for Stockton on Tees, Geoffrey de Freitas MP for Nottingham Central, and Arthur Blenkinsop MP for Newcastle East who was vice-president of the Ramblers Association.

Nancy Telfer was then 19 years of age. Now 80, she remembers the day well. "It was tea-time. All the shepherds were in, at the table. My mother put out the bread and cheese, sandwich cake and girdle scones, with home made butter and milk from the cow. All the usual things. It didn't make any difference that it was the important members of parliament. We were used to visitors. Hikers were always coming in. We didn't charge anything, wouldn't dream of it. Hugh Dalton was wearing his plus fours. You don't see anything like that nowadays do you? Geoffrey de Freitas, he was a really tall man, and he bumped his head on the clothes line above the fireplace."

The party then moved to Mr and Mrs Foreman's inn, the Rose and Thistle at Alwinton, where they spent the night. In a 1989 story recorded in the local publication, Clippings, John Philipson said that on the afternoon of the third day, they were met at Cottonshope Burnfoot, in Redesdale, where Lady Trevelyan "was waiting to drive us to Wallington, where we dined in their noble dining-room, in piquant contrast to the simplicities of our pilgrimage through the hills".

Left to Right: Barbara Castle MP, Hugh Dalton MP, Alec Tait shepherd with Mona Telfer aged 10, Nancy Telfer aged 19, Annie Telfer with daughter Jean aged 7 and her border terrier pup, Dawson Telfer, Andrew Watson shepherd, Neil Telfer aged 14.
Photo: From collection of Nancy Moscrop, formerly Telfer

71

Thus a second set of maps had to be produced, on exactly the same scale, with modifications marked. Whenever there was a dispute about the modifications, the county council staff would try to resolve them by discussion. When this failed, there would need to be a public hearing.

The much more straightforward process for the Borough and Urban Districts was summarised at the September 1955 council meeting. A total of 60 objections from 13 councils had been received. Among them, 23 had formed subject of hearings, 37 were resolved by discussion, 27 objections were admitted and 10 objections were withdrawn.[90]

By March 1956, all the objections to the Draft Maps for the Borough and Urban Councils had been resolved, and the Provisional Maps for those councils were proceeding.[91]

He made no bones about it the next stage. Starting with Morpeth and Belford, his staff were:

> … preparing for the more formidable task of settling objections to the Draft Map for the Rural Districts, so that the Provisional Maps can be prepared. It will take a considerable time to work through all the Rural Districts at the present rate of progress.

By June 1956, hearings for the Morpeth Rural District had taken place and were reported to the Footpaths Sub-Committee.[92] Mr J R Johnson, a member of the local bar, had presided at the hearings. Objections had been dealt with from the coastal parishes of Cresswell and Lynemouth to the agricultural areas as far west as Wallington. Of the 31 objections, Mr Johnson had recommended 12 deletions from the draft map, 14 should remain, 4 were modified, and one bridleway was reduced to a footpath.

A sad little note creeps in. Mr J R Bibby had made a representation that there should be a path from Mitford to Lowford Bridge, along the banks of the Wansbeck, but the inspector Mr J A Baldwin recommended that "no right of way be added to the draft map and statement".

Meanwhile the Ramblers were still adding new paths. In September 1956, the minutes record ten new representations in the sector leading down to Morpeth from the north west. They were in Todburn, Stanton, Netherwitton and Nunriding parishes. "The Sub-Committee are recommended to approve the inclusions in the Draft Map for Morpeth Rural District", records the minutes, and they did so.[93]

There were hearings about these new representations, presided over local member of the bar, Mr J D B Richardson. The report to the December 1957 committee shows three deletions, one to remain in the map, and one footpath to be upgraded to a bridleway.[94]

In May 1958, the Northumberland Gazette reported on a Footpath Inquiry at Longframlington, where over 50 local residents turned up.

> The footpath is part of an ancient way running from Felton to Rothbury, and the part contested is on the Ghyllheugh estate, owned by Major Rupert Milburn. Eighty-two year old Mrs Jane Robson said she used to live at Weldon Bridge and her husband walked the path daily to his job as a rabbit catcher.

Many other local people spoke out. Major Milburn was a serious objector.

This path eventually did survive, although with modifications, and the public do now have the right to walk along the southern bank of the Coquet, between Weldon Bridge and Pauperhaugh.

---

[90] Bridges and Roads Committee Minutes, vol 23 p 46
[91]   "   "   "   vol 23 p 107
[92]   "   "   "   vol 22 p 155
[93]   "   "   "   vol 23 p 204
[94]   "   "   "   vol 23 p 428 – 429

In September 1958, the county surveyor "has carefully considered (new) representations made by the Ramblers' Association for the inclusion of paths on the draft map "for various rural districts, including a new one in Morpeth Rural District. "His recommendations are based upon the evidence he has been able to obtain from local sources."[95]

Finally, in June 1959, the committee approved the Provisional Map for six Rural Districts, which included Morpeth. That would seem to be the end of the matter in our Rural District, but it is not quite the case. Major Milburn continued his opposition, which went to appeal. At its June meeting, the Footpath's Sub Committee was presented with a summary of the Appeal Court's decisions, including the Coquet riverside footpath:

> The path forms part of a continuous route on the south side of the river running west from Weldon Bridge. The path has been subject of two local inquiries and an application to the Quarter Sessions.

> The effect of the Appeal Committee's decision is that the public will continue to have a right of way from Weldon Bridge to Pauperhaugh on the south side of the Coquet but the route will avoid the Thistlehaugh Farm buildings.[96]

Finally by December 1960, the Definitive Map and Statement was submitted for Morpeth Rural District Council by the committee, and approved. The sigh of relief must have echoed throughout the countryside.

At County Hall, in Morpeth, all the maps from these days have been kept, in big files. They are at the scale of 6 inches to the mile, on the 1924 third edition Ordnance Survey map bases.

They show the field survey, the draft map, another one or two copies showing modifications to the draft map, and the provisional map. I went to look at them, to see if there had been any clearly lost paths, in the area leading down to Morpeth along the sector from the north and north west. Broadly speaking, the paths identified by the original parishes in the draft map are on our modern maps today, especially close in to Morpeth. One footpath from Newton Underwood to Newton Mill had been added at the provisional stage, and so had a bridleway south of Stanton Mill past Wood House, connecting with other bridle paths all the way to Throphill.

On a less happy note, an old footpath from Longhorsley to Hebron had its middle section cut out, between Fieldhead past Fenrother and Low Espley, a length of over two miles.

---

[95] Bridges and Roads Committee Minutes, vol 24 p 44
[96]   "   "   "   vol 24 pp 366 -381

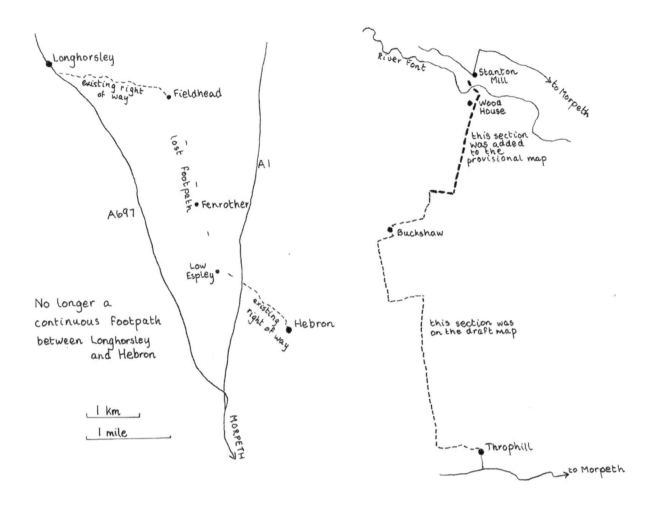

Meanwhile, the dramatic situation which would save the drovers' routes over the Otterburn Ranges was going on in parallel. The advertising of the draft maps in September 1954 for these areas caused a huge reaction.

The War Department gets a rather bad press from now on. They were adamantly opposed to rights of way in the inner firing sanctum of the Otterburn Ranges, which included Dere Street, and traditional paths down from there into the Coquet valley. They did not seem to oppose paths on the draft maps in the northern and eastern fringes of the ranges, including Clennell Street, The Street and Salters Road, which remained unmodified in the provisional map. The War Department's opposition thus was not quite the blanket version that it appeared to be.

Nevertheless, on Friday 17th August 1956, the Northumberland Gazette reported on a hearing at Alwinton, conducted by member of the local bar, Mr Lyall Wilkes. With the headline *Old Tales support freedom of hills",* the newspaper wrote:

> The inquiry was held at the Rose and Thistle Inn, reputed to be the secret hiding place of Rob Roy, and the 'locals', shepherds, farmers, clergyman, innkeeper, retired policeman and others – gathered in the old stone-built inn to press their claims to use paths and drove roads, some of which lead over the Border to Scotland. They claim the paths have been used for generations, and were at one time the routes for driving sheep and for bringing meal by horse and cart from over the Border.

The War Office, represented by their land agent Mr Thomas Charlton, however maintained that the paths were used for "occupational purposes and do not constitute public rights of way". Some 31 paths, the report says, are under discussion.

74

Among those who claimed their rights to use the paths were Thomas Carruthers, a retired policeman who had been a shepherd at Carlcroft in 1900; Mr Walter Little of Clennell, who had been shepherd at Blindburn and Carlcroft for 30 years, Geoffrey Foreman of the Rose and Thistle who was a veteran shepherd, and John Wilson, a retired Alwinton shepherd, who described how he travelled various paths as long ago as 1893.

The inquiry was adjourned and re-opened on 7th September. The Northumberland Gazette now ran the headline: *They want to keep the hill paths.* "This week they fought over every inch of them at an inquiry in the Rose and Thistle."

One of the "most interested participants in the fray was Mr Arthur Blenkinsop, Socialist MP for Newcastle East and National President of the Ramblers' Association."

The paper reported: "Col. Philipson of Harbottle pointed out that the Romans had used the paths; one known as The Street was actually part of the old Watling Street." Perhaps the paper's reporter was a bit confused here.

By March 1957, Mr Lyall Wilkes' report of the hearings was presented to the Footpaths Sub-Committee. Some objections had been settled without the need of a hearing, the county surveyor said, "as a result of discussions and further investigations by the County Surveyor and District Councils concerned". The report listed 91 paths in the Rural District of Bellingham, on the Otterburn Ranges. Of them, Mr Lyall had recommended that 51 be deleted, 33 should remain, 3 were modified with some deletions, and 4 were to be downgraded from bridleway to footpath.[97]

The committee approved and adopted the recommendations. But this was certainly not the end of the matter. The modifications were advertised, and then objections by the Ramblers and others resulted in further hearings.

In August 1957, the Northumberland Gazette reported on *The Border Battle for Footpaths*. There was a two day hearing at Harbottle, presided over by member of the local bar, Mr Johnson. Mr J Philipson, speaking as a member of the Ramblers' Association, was a principal objector to the War Department. He "maintained that the War Department prevented access to many Border paths and tracks".

Major T C Luke, a War Department land agent, explained:

> The range had been in use since 1914 and they had power to close all paths in gunshot range while firing was in progress, in the interest of public safety. Local people, he said, were mistaken if they thought the War Department was out to close all footpaths to the public. Their aim was to clarify the position – to establish which paths were public rights of way and which were not.

Among the other witnesses were shepherds, including eighty one year old Mr Adam Dunn, Mr John Wilson, and Mr Bill Dagg who was 79, all of Alwinton. Mr Dunn recorded that he and his father were shepherds in Yardhope for 72 years, and used many of the paths.

Mr Philipson said that one of these tracks was Gammels Path, where the Earls of Northumberland and Douglas met in 1401 to settle peace terms between Henry IV of England and Robert III of Scotland. The path was a common meeting place for wardens on both sides of the Border. It was one of the two main approaches to the Border hills, and formed part of Dere Street, the great Roman Road into Scotland.

He produced aerial photographs to show marks which archaeologists called "traffic ruts", proving that there had been heavy traffic along the road where it entered Scotland at Chew Green. This must mean animal traffic.

---

[97] Bridges and Roads Committee Minutes, vol 24 pp 288 - 295

A summary from the hearing was presented to the Footpaths Sub-Committee in December.[98] Mr Johnson obviously thought the objectors had a good case. The summary lists 33 paths to be inserted in the Provisional Map, six were to remain deleted, and one was to be modified with some deletion.

The report to the committee also said that "a number of representations by the Ramblers Association for the inclusion of paths in the Draft Map in this area had also been heard by Mr Johnson". There were 21 of these new representations. The sub-committee approved their inclusion.

Membership of the Ramblers Association was shooting up as a result of all this publicity. In February 1958, the Northumberland Gazette ran a short story about its AGM. The group stated that in 1957 of their total membership of 566, new enrolments amounted to 208:

> The major work in 1957 was the inquiry held at Otterburn and Harbottle as a result of our decision to contest the proposed deletion of many paths over the Redesdale ranges. This entailed extensive preparatory work, the briefing of counsel and attendance at the four-day hearing. We are pleased to record that a very good response was forthcoming from the public to our appeals for assistance.

On 16th March 1959, the Footpaths Sub-Committee approved the following, which refers back to the 21 new inclusions by the Ramblers.

> The Sub-Committee will remember that at their meeting on the 16th December 1957 they approved certain representations made by the Ramblers' Association for the inclusion of paths in the Rural Districts of Bellingham and Rothbury within the area of the War Department's Otterburn and Redesdale Ranges. The modifications to the Draft Map were advertised and an objection was made by the War Department to the inclusion of all these paths. Mr J R Johnson, a member of the local Bar, subsequently conducted a hearing at which both parties appeared. [99]

Of the 21 paths, Mr Johnson reported that all but one should remain in the map.

We are nearly at the end of the saga. By 13th June 1960, the county surveyor reported:

> The Sub-Committee will be pleased to learn that the final stage of the Survey has now been completed for the greater part of the County, and the Definitive Map and Statement, which the Sub-Committee are recommended to approve, are submitted for the following county districts."[100]

This list of districts did not include Rothbury and Bellingham, as these are the areas within which the still contested paths on the Otterburn Ranges lay.

The report stated that "the outstanding applications to Quarter Sessions in respect of paths shown on the Provisional map, of which the great majority have been made by the War Department, are expected to be disposed of by the end of the year".

It made clear that the Definitive Map and Statement are conclusive proof of the existence of public rights of way, but the fact that a footpath or bridle path is not marked on the map is not evidence to the contrary. It explained that a five yearly review will be made in which further paths can be added.

It went on to warn the committee that the War Department's application, which involved eighty five paths[101] over their Redesdale and Otterburn Ranges would be heard by a special court in September, and may take as long as a fortnight. The cost of the Counsel's brief was likely to

[98] Bridges and Roads Committee Minutes, vol 23 pp 430 - 434
[99]   "   "   "   vol 24 p 134
[100]   "   "   "   vol 24 pp 367 – 368
[101]   "   "   "   vol 24 p 368

be high, and payment would be required for the expenses of the large number of witnesses who may be called.

As predicted, the appeal took place in September 1960. One of the main witnesses was Mr J Philipson, who we will remember appeared at the earlier hearings. Surviving among his family documents from this time, which his family have been kind enough to let me see, is a small collection of newspaper cuttings, which allows us to pick up the details.

Army Seeks to Close Paths, reported The Times newspaper, on 20 Sept 1960. The Appeals Committee of the Northumberland Quarter Sessions:

> … were taken back to the thirteenth century with tales of border wars, appalling bloodshed and carnage; men as shaggy as the cattle they cared for, wolf trapping and excesses in remote moorland whisky houses.

> The War Department are asking that 93 paths should be removed from the county council's map which may be published next year. The Army at present operate a complicated and efficient warning system when the range is in use, and they have power to close the paths temporarily.

Mr W Steer for the county council described some of the paths such as Clennell Street, the "old drove road", the Swire, Dere Street which was an old Roman road and Gammel's Path.

Mr H A Taylor, the Northumberland county archvist produced maps and evidence dating back to the sixteenth century, including a book on the state of the frontiers written in 1550 by Sir Robert Bowes, Warden of the Eastern Marches. He also mentioned an inn known as Slyme Foot, where shepherds congregated for gambling and excessive drinking until the local rector discovered what was happening.

The Times reported that Mr John Philipson, secretary of the Newcastle Society of Antiquaries and a member of the Northumberland National Park planning committee, spoke of Clennell Street, Gammel's Path and the Golden Pots. Mr Philipson did not approve of the tone of the newpaper's report. Among the cuttings is a note which he typed:

> The Times Correspondent has highlighted the romantic aspects of the proceedings, and consequently, gives an inaccurate impression of their highly factual nature.

The Northumberland Gazette reported Mr Philipson as follows:

> He gave detailed quotations from ancient volumes, maps and documents referring to the paths, many of which are old drove roads used for moving cattle across the Border between England and Scotland in days gone by. The names of some of these paths have altered as the years went by, but the deep ruts made by the cattle as they were driven over the hills are plainly marked.

On the next day of the appeal, which was expected to last for two weeks, shepherds and hill farmers were the first of over a hundred expected witnesses to give evidence about the paths. The oldest was Mr William Glendinning, aged 81, who gave his profession as a sheep drover. He recalled journeys along many of these roads in the late nineteenth and early twentieth century.

Mr John Carruthers of Falstone, aged 71, said that he often met hikers, tramps and farmers, and he could remember the early days of the century when thousands of sheep would be brought from Scotland by the "Passpeth" to the sales at Rothbury.

Mr John Cobb, barrister for the War Department, cross-examined Mr John Philipson. He said that one of the paths that the county council was trying to preserve between Linbrig and "Passpeth" was only one foot wide in places, with a sheer drop to the valley below, and might be described as one of the most dangerous paths that could possibly exist. Mr Philipson replied that it was no more dangerous than Sharp Edge on Saddleback or Striding Edge on Helvellyn in the Lake District.

Mr James Rutherford, once a Coquetdale shepherd, said that he had seen hikers, fishermen, and "once I even seen a policeman" on Clennell Street. Mr Walter Dixon of Byrness had seen, as a boy, hundreds of tramps on these paths. They served as a means of bringing news to the remote farms.

The Northumberland Gazette lists others who gave evidence.
>   Mr Dawson Telfer of Uswayford
>   Mr Tom Carruthers, formerly of Harbottle
>   Mr Ralph Hedley of Whiteleas
>   Mr Walter Dixon of Byrness
>   Mr James Ferguson of Otterburn
>   Mrs J Philipson

Suddenly, and quite unexpectedly, on the next day the hearing came to an abrupt end. Mr Cobb said that a settlement had been reached after "delicate negotiations" and was "to give those that use these paths a substantial measure of liberty still to use them and at the same time to observe the needs of the War Department".

The county council spokesman told The Times:

> I think we have achieved a very satisfactory settlement and we have preserved the general rights of the public in the area for both the short and the long terms.

What was established has become the now well-known distinction between the Open Access Area and the Controlled Access Area. The paths to the east and the north of Upper Coquetdale:

> … will remain on the county council survey as rights of way. They include the routes known as The Street, Clennell Street and part of the Old Drove Road. The paths or sections of paths that cross the main firing area, including Dere Street, Gammel's Path and the Swire, are likely to be removed as rights of way.

The agreement had been reached overnight, during what seems to be hectic hours of negotiations, telephone calls to the War Department in London and the county council headquarters in Newcastle, and Mr C W Hurley, deputy clerk to the county council driving up to Rothbury.

Finally, there was an undertaking by the War Department that two paths, one from Linshiels to Foulplay, and the other from Harbottle to Stewartshiels, would not be included on the map, but that "the county council would be given the opportunity to re-dedicate them if at any time the War Department decided that they had no further use for the range".

On 29 September, The Times reported that the agreement came up at the Northumberland Quarter Sessions, who confirmed the terms of the settlement.

Mr Lavery, the Clerk of the County Council, wrote to Mr Philipson on 3 October 1960. He included this paragraph.

> I think it is significant that we have retained all the paths covered by the historical evidence and I feel that this result was due very largely to your intimate knowledge of the area and its history and your outstanding performance as a witness. I learned later that it was largely the weight of this evidence which eventually convinced the War Department that it was futile to contest many of the principal paths and encouraged them to seek a reasonable settlement.

He sent a map to Mr Philipson. In the course of writing this book, a family member has loaned me this map, and along with the cuttings from which the above extracts were taken, it is to be deposited soon at Northumberland Archives. The map shows the retained rights of way, and they included Gammels Path, Dere Street and many others on the western fringes of the firing range towards the River Rede, as well as those to the north and east of the range in the Coquet valley.

The lengthy procedure was almost over. On 12 December, the last of the Rural Districts' Provisional Maps, for Bellingham and Rothbury, were presented to the county council's Bridges and Roads Committee. The county surveyor reported:

> After a two-day hearing on the 19th and 20th of September, 1960, before the Appeal Committee of the Northumberland Quarter Sessions, a settlement was reached with the War Department whereby they withdrew their objection to the majority of the paths outside the immediate target areas on the Otterburn/Redesdale Artillery Ranges and undertook to replace two important paths crossing these areas if the land ceased to be used for defence purposes.[102]

The two paths which could be re-dedicated if the War Department had no more need for them in the future are described in great detail, section by section, in the county surveyor's report. They are a great loss, but perhaps some day in the future they may be returned to us.

The Battle of the Borders had been won by the local people. Like most battles, not every aspect had been a success. Two paths were lost for the foreseeable future, and it had taken a decade to get to this point. But it certainly was a case of democracy in action. Thanks to the initial passing of the National Parks and Countryside Act of 1949, the dedicated work of the councillors at all levels and county council staff, and the army of mainly anonymous volunteers, we can walk the paths of the drovers, the smugglers, the shepherds and the whisky drinkers for ever.

It is over fifty years since this process was concluded. Since then, the quest to keep footpaths and bridleways open, to upgrade and improve them has continued. The first review of the definitive paths in Northumberland took place in November 1963. By the time of the 1981 Wildlife and Countryside Act the system of countywide reviews at intervals was abolished and replaced by modification orders which could be made at any time.[103] At this time, the Ramblers' Association had compiled a list of over 100 footpath additions to be considered by the county council, which the footpaths officers tell me they have just about worked through now.

To the north and north-west of Morpeth, between the A697 and the Morpeth to Hartburn road, there are networks of minor roads, bridle paths and footpaths, most, if not all, of which in the past will have been used to move animals around, and often to bring them to Morpeth's market.

If we look at the modern maps, we can see some of the new paths which have been added near Morpeth, since the definitive map of 1960. From Todburn down to Doe Hill, a three mile bridle path has been added, crossing a new footpath which runs eastward from High Southward Edge.

Further east, some of the old paths, "horse-tracks or, at best, cart-tracks winding in and out through the fields from farm to farm", which appeared on the first Wallington estate map of 1728 were not put on the draft map. Neither did they appear on the new definitive map of 1960. Now however several have been added. There are bridle ways or footpaths from Fallowlees down to Greenleighton; from Harwood to Dyke Head and down to Gallowshill then on to Hartington, connecting with the Cambo Bridle Road in much of its ancient route. The intriguing track leading from Rothley Farm to Whitridge was not on the 1960 definitive map, but has re-appeared as a bridle way in the meantime. It would take a lot of time and hard work to identify those who have made all these changes.

---

[102] Bridges and Roads Committee Minutes, vol 24, pp 465 - 466
[103] John Riddall, p 89

Thus we have many people to thank for all their hard work. The Ramblers, the footpaths societies, the parish councils and concerned individuals and the hard-working rights of way team at the county council, all of whom have all helped keep the countryside open, and who still do.

One of the great successes of the rights of way legislation was the inclusion of the definitive paths on the Ordnance Survey maps. The information was gradually introduced onto the maps, in England and Wales, as it became available. The 1:50,000 Landranger maps in the pink covers and the 1:25,000 maps in orange or yellow covers all show the footpaths and bridle ways as rights of way, in England and Wales. They are all excellent for walkers, cyclists and horse riders.

The drovers found their way using knowledge gained from generations of experience, the younger learning from the older. We however have a different tool. Thanks to the dedicated campaigners of the past, and the easy availability of the Ordnance Survey maps showing the definitive rights of way, we have the freedom of the countryside. We can wave a map in our hands, and off we go.

THE LOST PATHS

The more northerly of the two lost paths runs eastwards from the Middle Golden Pot, following the Ridlees Burn downstream, past Ridlees Farm and Quickening Cote to Linshiels, where it joins the minor road to Alwinton.

Geordie Hall, who was born in 1916, lived and worked on the farms along the route of this lost path. In the book Coquetdale Camera, *he tells how his father and uncle clipped the sheep at Linshiels, but they would often go out and offer a day's clipping to another farm. "The wool from the outlying farms, such as the Ridlees and Ridleeshope, was brought down to Linbrig, where wagons would take it to Rothbury or Hawick."*

In the same book, there is a heart-touching photo of the handsome Ridlees farmhouse, of which nothing now remains. "The last occupants were the Hall family of Carshope, who lived there briefly during the winter of 1942 to 43. Older farmers still alive today remember walking their sheep to Rothbury market along this lost path, and would have known the occupants at Ridlees farm. The house and buildings were later used for target practice, and were finally bulldozed."

The lost path can be seen on modern Ordnance Survey maps, and on the Controlled Access Area maps produced for the public by the National Park and the MoD. It is still used by military vehicles, though the public has no access at any time.

The more southerly lost path runs from near Harbottle in a south westerly direction, passing to the south of East Wilkwood. Geordie Hall lived at there as a young man, between 1935 and 1940. He knew the family who lived there before him, Barbara and John Dunn and their six boys, John, James, Thomas, Ninian, William and Ralph. "The children lived too far away to go to school, and their mother taught them everything at home."

Coquetdale Camera *contains old photos of the lost farmhouses of East and West Wilkwood, with the families who lived in them. This path has disappeared from the Controlled Access Area map, and from the 1:50,000 Landranger map. On the Ordnance Survey 1:25,000 map, a slight track is marked heading that way.*

Photo: W P Collier, taken shortly before 1914.

My head is full of the language of droving, the holloways, the lairages and enclosures, the overnight stances where the cattle would be kept safely while the drovers enjoyed shelter and refreshment. I'm in Jedburgh, starting my third droving route over the Cheviots to Morpeth, and am interested to see that on the timetable the bus station is called Jedburgh Stance. Aha! Is this where the cattle stayed for the night in days gone by? I approach a bus driver. "Do you mind if I ask if you know why the bus station is called Jedburgh Stance?" I was hoping to get a juicy historical titbit about drovers, but he obviously thought this was a ridiculous question.

"Stance? That's what it means. A stopping place." So not just a place for drovers and cattle, but a word in everyday use in the Borders!

....

Along Dere Street to Towford
I'm at Cowhill, on Dere Street, a few miles from Jedburgh, where the ancient Roman road makes a sharp turn south for the Cheviot Hills. On the Landranger map, the spot is marked as Whitton Edge, but I like the name Cowhill, which reminds me of drovers, on the Cheviot Hills Explorer map OL 16.

Dere Street is the ancient Roman road along which the soldiers marched between Eboracum near York, over the border hills as far as the Firth of Forth. It passes close to the modern town of Jedburgh. It was constructed during the first Roman occupation of the Borders region under Julius Agricola from 70 AD, but it may have used the course of pre-existing tracks on at least some its route.[104]

This is one of the ways the drovers came, with their hundreds, their thousands, of black cattle from Scotland. Many of them were heading south to Stagshaw in the Tyne Valley, to Yorkshire and ultimately to Smithfield to feed the hungry capital. Some of them found their way to Morpeth, and I'm following in their footsteps. This time, I'm on my own, and a little nervous. I've got my bike and my tent, but there is some strenuous countryside to cross. I've timed it for non-firing days on the MoD Otterburn Ranges, and hope that I've got that right. The journey would take the drovers five or six days, and I'm planning to do it in two or three.

This point in Dere Street is 302 metres above sea level (NT 740190). There is a withered oak tree at the junction of paths, perhaps a landmark for olden day travellers in this grassy treeless landscape, and a wooden signpost showing the path ahead. Between the light grey stone walls, the track stretches down and onward, enticingly. Blue harebells are nodding among the ruddy grasses, along with hawkbit, yarrow and tumbling vetch.

Looking backward into Scotland, I can see the three Eildon peaks, near Melrose. The drovers who paused at this point would surely have taken a thoughtful look at the land they'd covered. Some of them would have come from the Highlands, the closer peaks of which I can just see in the hazy far distance.

I make my way southwards through a landscape surely as close to heaven as one can get on a sunny August day. It is open, wind free, fresh and grassy-scented. There are prehistoric remains, a stone circle called the Five Stones (NT 753168), some standing stones and a trestle cairn (NT 752161), although I don't know what that means. I have a real sense that this path was walked for millennia before the Romans and the drovers, and before me.

---

[104] Richard Carlton, p 36

Looking backwards into Scotland, from the trestle cairn on Dere Street

I'm heading for the Pennymuir Roman camps, near where I plan to make my overnight stance. Just before I reach there, I cross some fields where there is a herd of grazing Aberdeen Angus and Simmental cows with their calves. "Just gives the right atmosphere", I am thinking to myself. But Dere Street, that ancient route of inestimable value, has been churned up here by their feet making it almost impassable. I struggle to get through with my loaded bike. The half kilometre beside the forest plantation takes me almost an hour of exhausting lifting and slithering.

Once I'm past it, at the moorland crossroads there is a wooden pavilion. The fields adjoining are the site of the Pennymuir Fair. It was once a great sheep fair, flocks being driven from farms in the Cheviots and Borders hills. The fair still takes place on the first Saturday of September, and though smaller in scale, it is a living reminder of past ways in which people earned their living from the land.

I pass the Roman camps to Towford, a little further on. Here there is a wide green grassy haugh beside the Kale Water, where peaty water rushes over the concreted ford. I feel sure that this was an overnight or daytime stance for drovers. It is perfect, except for one thing. Midges! By the million!

Diving into my little tent, I examine my maps. Crossing the border from here over into England was one of the harder parts of the journey for the drovers, as it is for me. I'm heading for Elsdon village, which is about twenty miles away. Some of the way is steep and hard going, and was probably too far for the drovers to cover in one day with the cattle. For me, it is not practical to try to camp out on the military land, so I'll need to cross the ranges in one day.

The first destination is Chew Green Roman Camp. From Towford, there are two possible ways. One is to follow the Kale Water upstream as far as Nether Hindhope, then over Whiteside Hill and Coquet Head, joining the Pennine Way for a short stretch before dropping down to Chew Green. The other follows Dere Street, across Blackhall Hill and past the Roman Signal Station on Brownhart Law.

Towford to Chew Green, over Coquet Head
I decide to go over Coquet Head, which is a new route for me, and is surely a former drovers' route. Next morning, I follow the meandering Kale Water up the isolated valley as far as Nether Hindhope farm, along a quiet winding road. The 1899 Ordnance Survey map shows tracks marked as Drove Roads crossing towards the English border towards Hindhope and Chew Green. There is however no-one still living who remembers them.

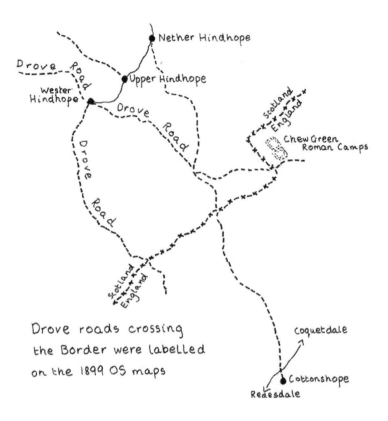

Drove roads crossing
the Border were labelled
on the 1899 OS maps

I talk to Mr Tim Elliot, the farmer at Nether Hindhope, while I'm checking my path. He didn't know anything about the marked drove roads, but he knew about driving sheep. He was born in 1938, which makes him six years older than me:

> Shepherds used to cross the border ridges from here, taking sheep to the sales at Rothbury, until the 1940s. All the farms in this valley and the Bowmont did it, often three hundred sheep at a time. It took three days. From Hindhope, they would go over Coquet Head to Chew Green, and then past the Golden Pots.
>
> From there, some of the shepherds would go down the Ridlees valley staying at Ridlees farm, and others would follow the Coquet valley down past Blindburn as far as Barrowburn. The second day, the flocks would pass Alwinton, and go as far as Sharperton. The third day they'd arrive at Rothbury, ready for the sales. They would go slowly, and the sheep would eat as they went. The shepherds always stayed on the farms. The sheep would be safe in the fields. They could eat and rest.

The route down the Ridlees valley is particularly interesting to me, as it is one of the lost roads of the Otterburn Ranges which will only return to public use if the army ceases to use the territory.

I follow one of the green tracks up between Hindhope Law and Whiteside Hill, pushing my bike. Grey clouds are approaching. Two motorcycles catch me up. I check my path with them. They are shepherd Allan Crozier and his grandson James. They come from Hindhope Shepherd House, even more remote than Nether Hindhope. The grandfather tells me that James, who looks about ten years of age, knows all the nearby hills really well, and that he is taking him a bit further afield so that he can learn more. He uses a motor bike to move around the farm because some of the hills are so steep it would not be possible on a quad bike.

They soon leave me behind. I am looking out for the earthworks marked on my map, and I see some, which seem similar to the cross dykes on Clennell Street. Once up on Coquet Head, the ground becomes boggy, and the grey clouds have descended. A heavy drizzle starts, accompanied by dense clouds, and it becomes hard to see the path. I nearly make a mistake when I find the Pennine Way signpost, as the path diverges. I am a little worried, but at some point the earthen banks of Chew Green Roman Camp appear through the drizzle, and I am able to re-orient myself. I know this is an easy route for young mountain bikers, because they have told me so, but these conditions aren't ideal for a grandmother with a push bike.

Towford to Chew Green, round Blackhall Hill
The alternative way to Chew Green follows Dere Street, and I did this stretch on a different occasion. From Towford, signs show Dere Street going straight uphill to a blocky looking building on the skyline, which is a shepherds' shelter with pens for working sheep. There is a round stone-walled field here, surely used for sheep gathering, but which has also been used for silage in the past.

More prehistoric sites are to be seen along the green track, with the great Iron Age hill fort of Woden Hill on the right, and several earthen banks looking like the cross dykes on Clennell Street. At Blackhall Hill, Dere Street either went round to the east, or along the steep western facing side. It is the latter which the sign indicates, but it is steep and narrow, and I find it hard to imagine Roman soldiers marching in rows along it. The path to the east seems much more practical. Once past Blackhall Hill, the heathery path leads to the border fence, and eventually to the border itself, passing the site of the Roman Signalling Station on Brownhart Law and down to Chew Green.

These four miles from Towford to Chew Green, on either route, would have taken perhaps half a day for the drovers with cattle.

Chew Green to Kyloe Knowe
There was a medieval settlement at Chew Green, and the road leading beyond it towards Elsdon was known as Gamel's Path. The earthen banks of the Roman camp may possibly have served as enclosures for cattle or sheep as the drovers passed through. Richard Carlton tells us:

> The remains of a building – still visible on a small haugh across the Chew Sike east of the Roman site - contain whisky bottles and other drink-related paraphernalia ... This suggests that Chew Green served as an overnight lairage for stock and a meeting place for drovers, served perhaps by a small resident population of farmers who may also have dabbled in other businesses close to the heart of drovers, such as blacksmithing and the procurement and sale of whisky.[105]

The same writer cites 13 spellings for Gamel's Path in documents from 1249 to 1601, and 16 map references with 11 different spellings dating between 1579 and 1825.[106]

I eat my lunchtime oatcakes and cheese standing up in the downpour, as there is no shelter anywhere, and then head up the steep slope on the now-surfaced road, towards the Golden Pots. Parallel with the road are intertwining holloways caused by the thousands of animals that passed this way over the centuries.

Chew Green to Kyloe Knowe
Tim Elliott, the farmer from Nether Hindhope, said that the shepherds on their way to Rothbury went over Coquet Head and down by the Golden Pots. These odd stone objects, with their fascinating name, were thus used as way markers even into recent times. They are actually cross socket stones, big strong stone bases with a hole in the middle in which tall crosses were stood. Now that the upright crosses have gone, the hole in the middle looks like a pot, and it catches rain water. Once their original use was forgotten, rumours as to what they had been must have abounded.

After going thoroughly through all the possibilities, Richard Carlton suggests:

> Golding Pottes would be a more appropriate name for a field containing some sort of pits, like 'Sand pottes, 'Colpottes', 'Claypots' etc... and it is more likely that Golding Pottes was the name

---

[105] Richard Carlton, pp 123 – 125
[106] Richard Carlton pp 38 - 40

85

given to a stretch of moorland near Dere Street, which had perhaps been scarred by some kind of extraction, and which, when deformed into Golden Pots, was subsequently transferred to ancient cross sockets alongside the road.[107]

The first one heading south after Chew Green is the Outer Golden Pot (NT 804072). The Middle Golden Pot is another mile further on, where the road from Cottonshope joins this one (NT 812063).

Outer Golden Pot

On this day, the weather has become so bad, and the rain is beating on me so incessantly as I cycle onwards that it is hard to know exactly where I am. I have over a dozen miles to cycle before reaching Elsdon. The deluge flattening me from above makes it impossible to get out my map or my compass, although I'm on the surfaced road so I can't get too lost. Then surprisingly a car pulls up. A young man with a German accent says they are looking for the way to the seaside on the west coast, going along the back roads. I certainly agree with them that that's what they are doing. They indicate to me the way they arrived here, on a road up from Elishaw, which I decide to follow. Once on the main A68, fearful of the traffic, I cycle to Otterburn, and order a taxi back to Morpeth. Yes, I know it is taking the easy way out. But some allowances may be made for my age, I say to myself.

So, although this is cheating a little, I'm back tracking a year to 2010, when I followed this route on a sunny August day. I'm cycling the same way, on the Great Drift Road, which became the name for this part of Dere Street, along which the cattle and sheep were driven between Chew Green and Elsdon.[108] Thousands of cattle moved along it, over the centuries, so that the surface of Dere Street became eroded and disappeared in many places.[109] The maps show several Roman camps along the way.

The great advantage of the Great Drift Road to the drovers was that it avoided the river valleys. It runs in a south easterly direction on the watershed ridge between the River Coquet to the north and the River Rede to the south. It doesn't need to cross any rivers or significant streams for the whole of this fifteen mile length.

The Great Drift Road departs from Dere Street near Featherwood farm. The Roman road drops down to Bremenium Camp at Rochester, in the Rede valley, but the drovers mostly stayed on the uplands. There is a long low east west sandstone outcrop here, marked as far back as the first edition 1860s Ordnance Survey map as Kyloe Knowe. The word *kyloe* refers to the black Highland cattle, and it looks like a place where the animals could have rested. On the 1:25,000 modern map, it retains this name, and the road running beside it is called Kyloe Road (NT 835042). Because the distance between Towford and Elsdon was likely to be too great a distance to walk in one day, this would be a good overnight stance. There is some shelter from the northerly and westerly winds among the rocks of the outcrop, and there are pools for watering the cattle nearby.

---

[107] Richard Carlton, pp 40 – 41
[108] Ian Roberts, p 65
[109] Ian Roberts, p 94

As I had been here in such impossibly drenching conditions, I wonder how the drovers managed. I come to the conclusion that, at natural resting places like this, too far from inns or villages, it is possible that they constructed simple shelters for themselves, acting like modern-day mountain refuge huts or bothies. Those with ponies perhaps brought their own portable shelters, but in such downpours, even putting up tents must have been fraught with difficulty. That ram's horn of whisky must have been very welcome in the long hours of the night.

Older maps show the road crossing in a south easterly direction from Kyloe Knowe, over the heather moorland, whereas now it swings round in a big semi-circle to the east and then south. The old route was shown on the Draft Map during the rights of way process in the 1950s, and it must have been subject to changes negotiated by the War Department then, or later.

The Otterburn Ranges

The next fifteen miles in the footsteps of the drovers are through some of the wildest, bleakest tracts of Northumberland's landscape. The Otterburn Ranges are used by the MoD and overseas armies for live firing. When the red flags are flying, the public is not allowed along the rights of ways which exist there, for obvious reasons. Non-firing days can be found by checking the MoD's website, www.otterburnranges.co.uk. It is a good idea to phone the friendly switchboard staff at Range Control as well, on 01830 520569. Sometimes there are last minute changes.

The ranges are in two sections, the Open Access Area and the Controlled Access Area. Both are within the Northumberland National Park. Very good leaflets showing cycling and walking routes are produced by the MoD and the National Park, and are easily available in National Park visitor centres. There are interpretation boards sited at focal points along the roads.

The landscape is unreal. Because it is controlled by the military, it is very tidy. There are no plastic-wrapped bales or rusting machinery, and no litter. The gates and cattle grids are smart and well functioning. At the same time, even though you must stay on the roads, there is a sense of how the landscape looked in the days of the drovers. When the army are not operating, which is when you will be there, it seems almost pristine. Strange and paradoxical indeed.

Kyloe Knowe to Elsdon

When I cycled along the Kyloe Road in August 2010, past Dudlees farm, I stopped at a viewpoint looking down on Elsdon village, near the site of the former West Fair Moor. I was cooking mushrooms I'd picked on the ranges, and soaking up the sunshine amid the smell of clover and hayfields. I hadn't read Ian Roberts' *The Drove Roads of Northumberland*, because it wasn't then published, but I'd read the Northumberland National Park's report by the same authors which preceded it. I was thinking about the importance of Elsdon to the droving trade.

Ian Roberts' book has much information and many photographs about this section of the road. Those who were heading for the great Whitsun or July fairs of Stagshaw[110] would bypass Elsdon, heading south towards Stagshaw Bank and the Tyne Valley. Others who were approaching Elsdon would pass the spot where I was cooking my mushrooms, and go along to the rear of the nearby toll cottage. Ian Roberts describes earthworks there, which show the parallel course taken by the drovers, keeping them separate from the turnpike road until they reached the village:

> Nowhere in Northumberland was droving more significant in the local economy than Elsdon … No less than three inns dating to the eighteenth and early nineteenth century are located around the green at Elsdon, although of the three - the Bird in the Bush, the Crown and the Bacchus

---

[110] Bailey and Culley, pp 172 - 173

(formerly the Scotch inn, a name which betrays its role) – only in the former is it still possible for the weary traveller to buy a drink today.[111]

On the 1731 Elsdon Enclosure Map, the sites of two fairs are shown, West Fair Moor and East Fair Moor. However after the turnpike roads of the 1750s, Elsdon's fairs seemed to lose out in importance. By 1839, the date of the Elsdon Tithe Map, the fair grounds are not shown.[112] Richard Carlton suggests that "they may have been made obsolete by Stagshaw, Morpeth and other stock markets in lowland Northumberland and beyond".[113]

Drovers going from Elsdon to Morpeth would need another two days' in which to complete the journey. This is the next interesting section for us to explore.

The Morpeth to Elsdon turnpike

The Morpeth to Elsdon turnpike gained its Act of Parliament in 1751. From Morpeth, it led past Mitford, Thropple, Longwitton, by the north side of Rothley Park Wall to Steng Cross, and to Elsdon's High Cross, a little way beyond the village. Armstrong's map of 1769 shows the road, but other than naming Old Barr near Hillhead, south of Elsdon, shows no turnpike gates.

Maps by Fryer, Greenwood and the first edition 1860s Ordnance Survey show no toll gates along the Morpeth to Elsdon turnpike, with the exception of one at Harwood Gate which served other turnpikes at the same point. Nor do any milestones appear. There are instead just four "guide posts", at Harwood Gate, Rothley Crossroads, near Longwitton and near East Thornton. This probably indicates that the turnpike was never a thorough success. The Morpeth and Elsdon turnpike trust had its final Continuance Act in 1801, and ended its operations in 1824. This is much sooner than other Northumbrian trusts which ended in the 1870s and 1880s.*

East of the site of Steng Cross, where the gibbet is now, Armstrong's map only marks the road with a dotted line, another sign that in the eighteenth century the turnpike may not have been very well maintained. The Bailey and Culley's map of 1794 shows no turnpike road between Rothley Crossroads and Morpeth.

The Hexham to Alnmouth turnpike shares the route of the Morpeth to Elsdon road for a mile or two, from Harwood Gate to Rothley Crossroads, as did the Newcastle to Jedburgh turnpike for a certain period. This section of the road is shown boldly on Armstrong's map. The Hexham to Alnmouth turnpike, in contrast to the Morpeth to Elsdon road, was well marked with milestones, many of which can still be found.

* W G Dodds. p 266

Elsdon to Rothley Crossroads

As travellers left Elsdon, they faced the long hard climb up the steep hill towards Harwood, where the gibbet now appears on the skyline. The gibbet is a modern reminder of a late eighteenth century murder. Steng Cross is just beside it, another of the cross socket stones in the same grouping as the Golden Pots. When the cross was standing, it would have been a prominent landmark for travellers, and the drovers who came this way would have known about it.

A mile past the gibbet, just past Harwood Head farmhouse, is a small stand of four sycamore trees. Nothing else. Just four trees. This is the site of The Shop (NT 978903), named as such on the 1769 Armstrong map. It was a former blacksmith shop, and a very significant part of the story of drovers on their way to Morpeth and Newcastle.

---

[111] Ian Roberts, pp 64 – 67 and 99 – 108
[112] Elsdon Tithe Map, 1839
[113] Richard Carlton, Illustration 33, Elsdon Tithe Map

The Shop Trees on the road from Elsdon (NT 978903)

We know about it because the Women's Institute at nearby Cambo compiled a collection of oral memories of rural life, published as a book in 1929 called *In the Troublesome Times*.[114] Here are the words of Edward Keith:

> In pre-railway days, when great droves of cattle were driven over the Carter into these northern counties, it was usual to have them shod with plates of iron, to prevent the animals falling lame when travelling great distances over rough, gritty turnpike roads. Up to about eighty years ago a flourishing blacksmith's business – employing three to four men – was carried on right up on the Harwood moors, about a mile from Winter's Gibbet on the Elsdon road. As the Chevy Chase coaches and lines of carriers' carts used this road between Jedburgh and Newcastle, up to the building of the new road between Belsay and Otterburn, the shoeing business must have been a heavy item; but it is no less a fact that this shoeing of cattle was the leading line in the business.

Other commentators in the book confirm this account, including butcher Adam Wilson:

> I have butched three that were shod. The shoe was in two parts so that the hoof could divide, otherwise they could not have walked. I have one of the old shoes.

Shoeing cattle? I'd never heard of such a thing until I started reading books about droving.

A R B Haldane describes it. The Scottish drovers met the difficulties of the gravel of the new roads by shoeing the beasts, particularly in autumn or bad weather:

> The method of shoeing cattle was rough, for the beasts had to be thrown on their backs, often with serious damage to the horns, the head being held down and the feet tied while the shoeing was being done. The shoes used by the drovers for their cattle were thin metal plates, crescent-shaped and nailed on the outer edge of the two hooves of each foot with fine metal nails the heads of which were formed of cross pieces giving the nail the appearance of a small hammer. A beast fully shod thus required eight metal plates, but it seems that often only the outer hoof of each foot was shod, as the most wear came on this outer edge.

He writes that the shoeing of half-wild cattle fresh from Highland grazings and unused to handling must have been difficult work, but a smith of Aberdeenshire once shod as many as seventy cattle in a day, probably shoeing only the outer edge of each hoof.[115]

---

[114] Rosalie Bosanquet ed, pp 180 - 181
[115] A R B Haldane, pp 32- 35

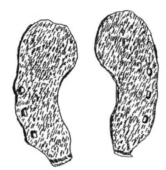

The cattle shoes were in two parts for cloven hooves, and about 3 inches or 8 centimetres long.

Sketch adapted from A R B Haldane's Drove Roads of Scotland

Links between the Cambo area along the drove routes to and from Scotland are remembered too in the Cambo recollections. Mr Charlton:

> The farmers from about here used to go up to Falkirk Fair to get their Kyloes, and Mrs Hall of Scots Gap's brother was one of those who used to be engaged to go and drive them down.

This rare surviving anecdote illustrates that it was not only Scottish drovers bringing cattle this way, but that farmers also went north to buy cattle, and bring them back. Falkirk was the site of the principal fair for Scottish cattle, from 1770 onwards. The numbers of cattle they sold were huge. At its peak, in 1827, 130,000 cattle and nearly 200,000 sheep changed hands.[116] The memories of the Cambo villagers, or of stories told to them by their parents or grandparents, stretched back as far as the 1840s.

Nowadays, the blacksmith's forge at the Shop Trees is nothing but a memory. Although local people say that people with metal detectors have found cattle shoes there, no-one that I've asked has been able to tell me where I can see one.

Beyond the Four Trees, the road to Morpeth then passes Harwood Gate. The name records the toll gate here, where "travellers had to pay to get through", loosely attributed to Miss L Davison below:

> It used to be very busy at one time. Many people gathered there because there were tilesheds close by at Gallowshill, where there is a plantation; they made pipes for draining the fields; it was the time when so much draining was being done; and the lime kiln between Hartington and Gallowshill was working; and these employed a great many men. Droves of cattle used to be driven past, and there were carriers' carts and farmers' carts.

The actual function of toll collecting at Harwood Gate is a bit mysterious. At different times, up to three turnpike roads passed through the one toll gate. The mind boggles as to how the tolls were sorted out. Harwood Gate is shown as a toll bar on Fryer's 1820 map, but it does not appear on Greenwood's map of 1828 or the first edition 1860s Ordnance Survey.

The farm called Donkin Rigg near here is spelled Duncan Rigg on Armstrong's map. In his short book, *The Alemouth or Corn Road*, Morpeth historian Harry Rowland wrote that "before the railway came, this was the assembly place for cattle being driven to Newcastle or Morpeth markets – this was perhaps the last stage on a long journey".[117] That busy landscape full of working people is now one of the bleakest landscapes imaginable.

At the time of the Wallington estate map of 1728, before the turnpike and the improvements made by Sir Walter Blackett, this was a landscape of bog and moorland where the droves from the Great Drift Road would meet those crossing the Simonside hills, coming along the Cambo Bridle Road, and from Chartners.

---

[116] A R B Haldane, pp 220 - 221
[117] Harry Rowland, p 38

Elsdon to Rothley Crossroads through the forest

There were other possible droving routes from Elsdon to Morpeth. To the east of the village, not far from the former East Fair Moor are Hudspeth, Landshott and Whiskershiel farms. Further on are East Nook farm and Whitlees, where there is an old bastle among the outbuildings. Between here and Rothley Crossroads is a great expanse of modern forestry. This area has interesting historic features tucked among the trees.

Whitlees bastle, in Harwood forest

Hughie and Margaret Mather live in Harwood village, deep in Harwood Forest. Hughie gave us the story earlier of the machinery which sank into the bogs. Just as the drovers and pack horse leaders crossed the Simonside hills with their animals, Hughie thinks nothing of cycling through the rolling forested land along the bumpy tracks all the way to the car parks near Lordenshaws. He gave me tips on how to do it. His cycling exploits serve as a reminder that this moorland landscape between here and the Coquet valley is one connected land mass.

Now that much of this area is forested it takes more imagination to picture the herds moving along, except in evocative clearings such as at Redpath (NT 004926), where the farmhouse still survives. Manside Cross is another of the cross socket stones, which has part of the stone shaft surviving in it. Historic records tell us that the shaft was probably reused in post medieval times as a boundary stone, as it is carved with modern initials.[118] It is sited next to a rectangular Iron Age settlement, and near an OS pillar showing 325 metres elevation (NT 984921). Hidden in the forest, they are a reminder that this route is an ancient one, and it goes to Morpeth.

Harry and Amy Scott of Otterburn have an old map of Elsdon hand painted onto linen fabric. From Whitlees a definite track is marked "to Morpeth", and it heads straight for Manside Cross. A footpath is marked on the modern maps along this track, through the forest.

Harry was born in East Nook farm in 1937, and he spent all his life in the farms in this area. He had some droving stories:

> My father and mother used to drive sheep from East Nook to Scots Gap, to the mart. There was no forest on Whiskershiel Fell then. They drove them through the Harwood forest area, to Ralph Shield, where they would put the sheep in a field, and walk the four miles back home. Next day, they'd walk back, and drive the sheep the rest of the way to Scots Gap, about the same distance. Yes, they probably paid a little bit to leave the sheep overnight.

---

[118] www.keystothepast, ref no N9781

In 1962, my parents moved farms, from East Nook to Catcherside on the Wallington estate. We moved the beasts ourselves. We got together with a few neighbours, three or so of them on horseback. We drove about 50 cows with calves, and yes, likely, a bull. There was a path through some of the young forest. We crossed the road by Harwood Head, and over the moor past Birkyburn. The cows tend to hurry along at first. Then they get a bit tired and realise they are going to be driven, so they settle down to a steady pace. We wouldn't take dogs. Cows with calves would get too excited. The men on the horses were there so that if one or two of the stock ran away, they could be rounded up easily. There were no wagons then. That was the way you had to do it.

Rothley Crossroads to Morpeth

Once at Rothley crossroads, travellers going to Morpeth could follow the course of the turnpike road through Longwitton, or they might choose any of a series of lanes passing through Scots Gap, Middleton, Hartburn and Mitford, some of which are now minor roads, bridleways or footpaths.

William Brewis was farmer who lived along this way. Between 1833 and 1850, he wrote a diary, and he told us the story about the elopement to Coldstream Bridge.[119] He lived at Throphill, five miles from Morpeth, and regularly went to the Wednesday market. His diary often recorded the price of beef and mutton per stone:

> Wednesday 22nd February 1837: Beef 6/6 to 7/-, mutton 8/- per stone, a full market of beef but sheep dear.

> Wednesday 14th June 1837: A full market of stock beef 8/-, mutton 7. A good many cattle, bullock, Scotland.

In those days, 6/6 meant six shillings and sixpence, 7/- was seven shillings, and there were twenty shillings to one pound. A stone weighed 14 pounds.

He attended Morpeth hiring fairs, where he would engage servants and farm labourers. During the week 28th June to 4th July 1847, he wrote about going to Stagshawbank Fair:

> I intend being at Stagshawbank Fair on Monday, and leaves at 2 o'clock today 4th to be at Stamfordham all night, will make it easier for tomorrow in a Gig, taking a servant with me to drive the Cattle home, I have sold all my wintering Cattle both Oxen and Queys at an early period, which makes me in want of a fresh lot. I am doubtful they will be bad to purchase, at least those that are very fresh, the severe winter and the failure of the Turnips in spring is the cause of all this.

The animals he bought and sold at Morpeth would have been driven along the road from Throphill through Mitford. The closer he got to the town, as the routes come together from all directions, the busier it must have been, especially on the days before and after the market. There must have been many an interesting conversation between the long distance drovers with their Scottish voices and the local Northumbrian farmers.

There were several public houses servicing people moving along the Wansbeck valley. Some survive to this day, like the Ox at Middleton, the Fox and Hounds – now called the Dyke Neuk - where the turnpike from Longwitton is on a sharp bend, and the Plough at Mitford. The Beehive at Hartburn is only a memory.

Suddenly, in 1862, droving of animals along this stretch changed. The Wansbeck Valley Railway, later the North British Railroad, ran its first train on 23rd July, between Morpeth and Scotsgap.[120] From then on it carried sheep and cattle to Morpeth, as well as passengers and freight. Behind the locomotive would be the passenger carriage, and often behind that two or three wagons containing livestock.

---

[119] William Brewis, pp 25 - 30
[120] Alan Young, pp 97 - 100

Lancelot Robson has lived in Hartburn virtually all his life. Born in 1916, he remembers the Wansbeck valley line:

> The railway was important to the local farmers, who invested in the North British Railroad when it was set up in the 1860s, so as to be able to transport their animals to the markets, especially to and from Morpeth. When my grandmother died in 1932, she left thousands of £1 paper shares in a chest. Instead of using the roads, each farm would have a track down to the railway line or the railway station. My father would drive his animals down to Middleton station from Greenside, where we lived. Other farmers would come to the station from places like Todridge and South Middleton.

Farmers were able to contact the station master at the station closest to the farm, order a wagon, load it on the day of travel and it would then be attached to the first convenient train.[121]

From Scots Gap, the stations along the Wansbeck Valley line were at Middleton, Low Angerton, Meldon, and finally Morpeth. From the junction at Scots Gap, trains ran to Rothbury and to Bellingham via Reedsmouth. All of this is now only a memory, the almost-forgotten Wannie Line.

It's been a long and ever changing story, of those who have passed over the hills and along the valleys, following the border routes from towns like Jedburgh, Kelso, Coldstream to Morpeth. There have been prehistoric hill dwellers and Roman soldiers; Highland drovers with their kyloes; drovers like George Robson with their shorthorns and sheep; and then the farmers of the nineteenth and twentieth centuries who put their animals on the steam train, itself passing into history when the line finally closed in 1952.

---

[121] Ian Roberts, p 85

Photo: Reproduced with permission of Beamish Museum, and help from Morpeth Antiquarian Society

This is a surviving and unusual photograph of sheep being driven in Morpeth, along Newgate Street past Bullers Green. Taken in the early years of the 20th century, it is printed from a lantern slide in the collection at Beamish museum. The drover or shepherd is moving the sheep along, steering his bicycle in his right hand. If we look closely at the background, there is another flock of horned sheep following the first, and the drover appears to be on horseback. The flocks are being carefully kept apart.

George Robson's personal account from the late eighteenth and early nineteenth century is an exceptional survival of a drover's tale. There are people still living however who can tell us about droving in Northumberland in the twentieth century, or whose parents or grandparents told them stories. These are rare and precious accounts.

Most of them tell of driving sheep to market towns on both sides of the Cheviots, such as Rothbury, Wooler, or Hawick.

George Murray Anderson

George Murray Anderson wrote a book called *From the Glen to the Lowlands*, when he was 85. It was published in 1979. He was born just over the Border near Carter Bar, in Roxburghshire, in 1894. In 1910, they lived at Attonburn, on the Scots side of the Cheviots in the Bowmont Valley. When he and his brother were aged 16 and 14, they were sent to drive 300 lambs over the Cheviot hills to Midgie Ha', in Northumberland, a few miles from Hepple and Holystone. From his book, we learn not only details about the drove, but the extent to which young lads were trusted in those days.

They left during the middle of July, just before the heather came into full bloom. Heather was a complete change of diet for these lambs, he explains. Previously they had been grazed on rich, green grass and also had their mother's milk. The idea was that the change of food would act as a cleansing of the system. There were no drugs available in those days to destroy the various internal pests which attacked sheep:

> So Frank and I were instructed to drive these lambs right across the Cheviot Hills. The first night we stayed at Cocklawfoot. Next day, we set off up the face of the Cocklaw. When we got to the top the ground was reasonably level but boggy and it was very rough going. We then crossed the boundary on to the large hill farm of Uswayford and after another hour or so we saw the farmhouse and the buildings away off to the left. Eventually we came to the Usway River; the water was dark, the colour of strong tea, coming from the peat bogs on the higher reaches.
>
> After crossing the Usway River we saw a big pole standing alone on up on the hillside. We had been told to look out for this pole, known as the Guide Post. So we soldiered on and eventually came to the only other house we had seen, a shepherd's cottage called Wholehope. We had still three miles to go to the next house, Clennel Street, also a shepherd's house, where we left the lambs for the night in a field surrounded by a dry stone wall. Less than two miles brought us to the Red Lion Hotel in the small village of Alwinton where arrangements had been made for us to stay the night. After we and our dogs had dined, it was nice meeting some of the kindly folk of the village.
>
> Next morning we were on our way again with our drove. I shall never forget that scorching hot day and the flies attracted by the sheep. Leaving Harbottle, we seemed to make slower and slower progress in that sultry sun. At last we turned off the main Rothbury road at Wood Hall and a little further on we came to Holystone where there is a heathery common. We were glad to rest the lambs and call at the inn to be out of the sun for a time at least.
>
> It was about 4 p.m. on that blistering afternoon that we eventually arrived at Midgie Ha', all very tired and weary. Mrs Glendinning had been doing her washing that day; being of stoutish build and rather more than middle age her jolly face showed signs of the great heat that she had endured. I remember her saying in her rich Northumbrian accent 'If weather is going to continue like this I must get washing up-a-height', meaning up the hillside where the air would be cooler.
>
> Tea included Mrs Glendinning's home-baked bread and scones, and home-made butter and jam; the dogs too were not forgotten. Mr and Mrs Glendinning were exceedingly kind people.
>
> Next morning I set off to walk back home, leaving Frank in charge of the 300 lambs on some 1,500 acres of heather with unfenced boundaries. If the lambs got away they could wander for many miles and Frank put in a very anxious and strenuous 14 days shepherding. He had to be

95

with the lambs from daybreak otherwise they would start wandering – a tough job for a boy not yet 15 years of age.

So with crook, and dog at foot, I carried on homewards. The great heat of the previous day had gone and a slight breeze was blowing just right for walking on the hills.

Frank managed to bring the lambs back home by himself, the only misfortune being a dead lamb, bitten by an adder as they moved across Holystone Common. At the end of the second day as he started to descend the Cocklaw a severe thunderstorm broke overhead, with continuous vivid flashes of lightning, immediately followed by terrific cracks of thunder. This must have been very frightening indeed, especially to a boy of his age up on the heights of the Cheviots with 300 lambs as his responsibility and his poor dog becoming petrified with fright. I have no doubt Frank was most thankful when he eventually reached Cocklawfoot.[122]

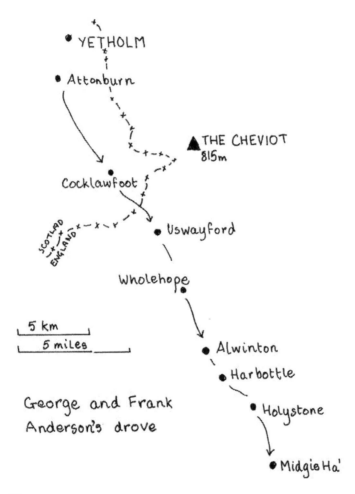

George and Frank Anderson's drove

George Murray

George Murray, of similar name to George Murray Anderson above, was born in Hawick, Scotland, in 1891. His story and the next are from oral history recordings in the Northumberland Archives.[123]

His parents were Scottish, and they worked in Northumberland, in the Kielder and Alwinton areas. They moved to Uswayford in 1912, Rowhope in 1914, and Barrowburn in 1927. His wife was born in Barrowburn in 1900. These farms are all in the Upper Coquet valley.

The recording was made in 1974, when he was 83 years old. Among his stories are tales of constant movements with the sheep after the family moved to Uswayford, during September and October, 1912. There usually seemed to be about 100 sheep per shepherd. He tells how

---

[122] George Murray Anderson, pp 28 - 34
[123] George Murray, Audio Tapes 62 and 63, Northumberland Archives

they took 450 ewes to the sale in Rothbury. Then they took 480 to the heather moors at Hagdon, a total distance of nearly 40 miles.

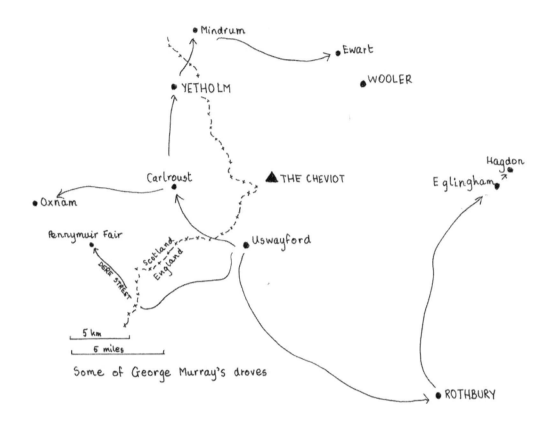

Some of George Murray's droves

In November, they collected 300 sheep from the hill. They drove them over the Cheviots to the Scots side, 100 to Oxnam, 100 to Mindrum and 100 to Ewart. They took them to the Leicester rams in those places, and left them there for about three weeks, by which time most of the ewes would be in-lamb. And then they collected them again.

He relates a three day drove to Ewart. The first day was from Uswayford to Carlroust. The second day was from Carlroust to Mindrum, and the third day from Mindrum to Ewart. Then they brought tup lambs from Ewart to back to Mindrum, and put them on turnips for the winter.

Sometimes they took sheep to the September Pennymuir Fair, along Dere Street.

As the shepherds moved around, they stayed overnight at farms. We can imagine that it was not like modern farmhouse bed-and-breakfast accommodation, with freshly laundered and ironed sheets and en-suite bathrooms, or three course evening dinners. Sometimes, he said, the shepherds would stay out with the sheep all night. There were so many that they had to watch them.

The blackface sheep, he said, did well on the heather lands, and the Cheviot sheep on what they called the "white land", the hill grassland. "We took the sheep from the white land to the heather for two weeks. This did them the world of good. Nowadays we dose them." This would explain the long walk to the heather at Hagdon.

When the interviewer asked him what the women did, he said that "the cows were up on the hill then. The women had to go up to milk them, and bring the milk down. They were busy setting potatoes, weeding them, taking them up. The families were more self sufficient then."

Eddie Bertram

Eddie Bertram was born in 1906, and interviewed in 1978.[124] He was only fifteen when he did his first drove, from Broadstruther on the north eastern side of the Cheviot, to Alwinton. Many of the following stories are about the time he worked as a shepherd for Captain Leyland, at Kidlandlee, beyond Alwinton in the Upper Coquet Valley. He said that Captain Leyland owned eight farms, and had eight flocks of sheep:

> There were no lorries then. Ye had to drive them. Once a fortnight to the sales, from August to early October. Ye would start two days before the sale, it depends how far ye had to drive them. They would all be marked blue or red. They would be sold in batches of 50.

> All the wether lambs, that's the castrated males, would go. Ye would draw out the best ewe lambs for your own farm, and sell the rest. They were called the *shotts*.

> Then the draft ewes would be sold, at six years or sometimes five years old. The lowland farmers bought them and crossed them with a blue Leicester, for the mule lambs.

> We would drive right over Cheviot with the lambs, to Wooler. The flocks would be a quarter of a mile behind each other. There would be so many sometimes that the sheep would get all mixed up, and there was some language then!

> Our first stop was Langleeford. We stayed all night there, put the sheep in some fields. Next morning ye set off, and ye drove into Wooler. The lambs were put into different fields in Wooler. Ye went and lifted them in the morning and they went straight into the sale pens.

> After the sale, when we went back to the Coquet, there was a little bus used to take us, and there generally was a lot noise, especially among the older ones. In fact some of them didn't get back until about two days after the sales.

> Old Dodd Anderson, he was my mother's cousin, they were going over the River Alwin one night, and of course they always had the bottle with them. And there were these stepping stones, and Old Dodd, he slipped and fell on a stone and broke the bottle. And he got to the other side on his hands and knees shouting 'Drink ye bugger drink.' They would go on the binge after the sale, but then they wouldn't have another drink for months.

> Sometimes I would drive from the Head of Coquet to Longhorsley, and back again. A solid week's droving. The first stop was Netherton. We had a park there. Then down by Rothbury, where you got some of the mart fields. Then up Garleigh Moor and over the Lee to Longhorsley. Stayed the night at the Shoulder of Mutton. That was the longest drove I ever did.

> The worst drive ever, I was set away in the month of May with ewes and lambs only four to six weeks old. I was set away from Milkhope and then I got to Netherton, and I was to go to Rothbury. I was absolutely beat. The lambs were dead beat. Walter Brown the head shepherd said to me: 'Ye'll stay the night at Netherton.' The sheep lay down, completely jiggered. I took fifty ewes with twin lambs on that one.

> The grass parks in Ewart were let in spring by auction. £60 or £70 per acre, March to November. Ye had to take the sheep out in November. In the grass parks, ye got a shepherd to look after your stock.

> After the Rothbury sale, trains were leaving every half hour until three o'clock in the morning. Buyers came from Durham, Yorkshire and Cumberland.

> The biggest drove I ever had to do was 39 score. We left Whiteburnshank and Fairhaugh, Leyland's sheep. There were three shepherds when we took them away. We drove them onto Simonside Hill, onto the heather. We took them to the heather for ten days or a fortnight – did them the world of good. We used to pay a ha'penny a head a week.

> On the day we were due to come home, it absolutely poured down. Old John Oliver who farmed part of Simonside Hill said: 'Don't take them away today'. So we stayed an extra day.

---

[124] Eddie Bertram, Audio Tape 127, Northumberland Archives

But the two shepherds who were to meet me, to help take them back didn't turn up, so I had to take them on my own.

As soon as I let them through the gate, the sheep knew exactly where they were going. They just left by themselves. I was behind, helping the stragglers, and one or two lame ones. When I was two miles this side of Harbottle, I met old Doctor Bedford. He had his car pulled into the roadside to let the sheep by. I said: 'Where's the front of the flock?' He said: 'They're making their way through Harbottle.' That is, the flock was two miles long, the sheep going by themselves. When I got to Alwinton, they had gone up to what we call Clennell Street. I was on my own. They were racing away up back there, back to Kidlandlee.

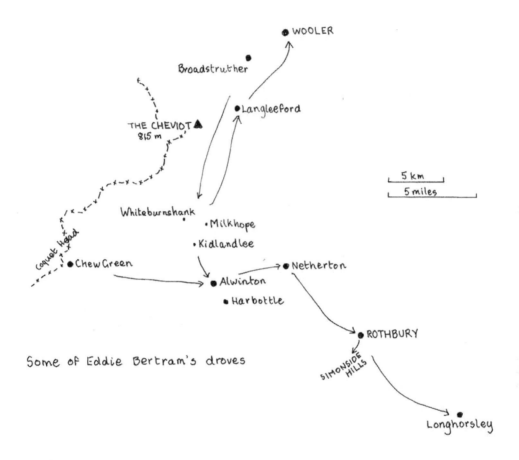

Some of Eddie Bertram's droves

Jean Foreman and Nancy Moscrop

Jean and Nancy are two sisters who lived at Uswayford as children. This is one of the most isolated farms in the county, and to this day several miles from a tarmac road. Mary and I met Jean when we arrived in Alwinton, after our crossing of Clennell Street.

Jean Telfer was born in 1943. She married Angus Foreman, the publican at the Rose and Thistle in Alwinton, where she still works in the family business:

> All the farmers would bring the sheep down from the hills to Alwinton, and rest them on the village green while they went in to the Rose and Thistle to have a pint. Then they drove the sheep to Rothbury. One would go in front to keep an eye open for cars. Then the sheep would go, with the shepherd behind, and one or two dogs to each shepherd.
>
> From Uswayford it would take two days to Rothbury. They would rest on common land at Sharperton Haugh, below the bridge. At Rothbury, the marts owned the fields, in the haughs beside the river, before the town.
>
> The start of motor traffic made life difficult sometimes. Ted Cowens from up the valley got wrong when a car ran into the sheep he was driving. He had to go to court, for not having someone in

front of the sheep. The other shepherd hadn't been available. He said in court: 'Aa war not Jesus Christ. My sheep wadna follow me!'"

Jean sent us on to her sister, Nancy Moscrop, who now lives at Holystone:

I was born in 1938. When I lived at Uswayford, while I was still at school, there were three hired shepherds. There were ten people in the house after Jean was born, five children, three shepherds, and our mother and father. The shepherds slept in one room, a double and a single bed. They stayed with us until 1962, when my parents left Uswayford.

I left school when I was fourteen, and for the first two years I helped around the house and with the lambing, things like that. When I was sixteen, I started work as a shepherd. I went on the payroll. I did everything. Sometimes, I used to drive sheep from Uswayford to Alwinton, across the boundary, through what we called the Five Gates, between Uswayford and Whiteburnshank farms, on the Yarnspath Law. There were so many sheep that we got them through more quickly, with the five gates open.

We joined Clennell Street just before Wholehope. It was a shepherd's cottage at the time. The ones I drove were going to the market at Rothbury, 40 or 50 at a time. We'd have a couple of dogs. I'd take the draft ewes. They were the old ones. It was seven miles along the hilltop road from Uswayford to Alwinton.

I stayed on Alwinton farm, with my auntie Minnie. Many a time I stayed there with her. She'd married James Waddell, same Waddells as had Otterburn Mill. The sheep rested in the flat fields next to the Alwin on the road to Clennell, on the left side.

When we lived at Uswayford, there would be a gathering on the high Cheviot after the clipping, in July. We would take the strays up. It was a meeting place. The shepherds from Cocklawfoot would bring theirs up. Dad would go, or one shepherd. They sorted out the sheep.

The shepherds also used to drive the sheep to High Bleakhope, over Bloodybush Edge. There was a sheep track between the farms. This is what they call the Salters Road. The sheep would go back and forward. Henry Kelly was the farmer who employed us at Uswayford, and he also had High Bleakhope. Sometimes the High Bleakhope sheep would come to us for lambing, because we had more shepherds, and they'd be to drive back when the lambs were big enough. They did it many a time.

Sometimes the drovers came from Scotland. There was Adam Scott. He called married women *mistress.* We all called him Yid. He was from Scotland from a farm we called the Uplaw, spelled Wooplaw. He walked his sheep to the heather at Midgie Ha', because our farms were on the 'white ground', that is grass, and on the way back he spent quite a lot of time at the Rose and Thistle. Then he stayed overnight with us at Uswayford. He would just find a bed in the house where he could.

It was usual in those days to walk back and forth over the hills. Mrs Little from Cocklawfoot would walk over the border four miles to Uswayford on Sunday, to have her tea with us. And then she'd go back again. She had plenty of lads, five in fact. They'd come over to help with the clipping. The wonder is that none of us married any of them, with us being four girls at Uswayford. Often the lads would walk over to the dance at Windyhaugh, and then stop the night at Uswayford on the way back.

The photo on the next page shows Nancy Telfer with Laddie in 1952, when she was a working shepherd aged 21.

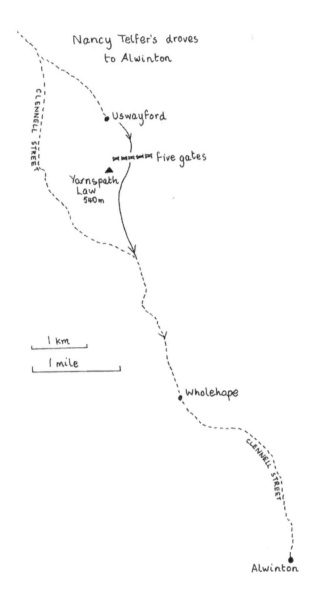

Nancy Telfer's droves
to Alwinton

CLENNELL STREET

● Uswayford

⊢⊢⊢⊢ Five gates

Yarnspath
Law
540m

1 km

1 mile

● Wholehope

CLENNELL STREET

Alwinton

Over Yarnspath Law

When Nancy was driving her sheep over Yarnspath Law, she may have been following an ancient route.

"Clennell Street is first record as Yarnspeth or Ernespeth in deeds relating to the holdings of Newminster Abbey, near Morpeth, during the late twelfth century, when it formed one of the boundaries between Clennell and the Kidland Forest, suggesting it was then an ancient routeway and boundary. The first known mention of this route in written documents is in Odinel de Umfraville's charter of 1181, in which the boundaries between Kidland and Clennel are defined."

Richard Carlton, p 41

After Nancy married in 1954, she and her husband lived at Girsonfield near Otterburn. She helped with the sheep all her life, even doing the lambing entirely by herself when her husband had a hip replacement. "Once you know how to do it, you never stop," she said. "I went on until we retired in 1993."

Jane Ellen Hall

We've learned a lot about droving sheep and cattle, but Jane Ellen Hall drove geese. She was the mother of Geordie Hall, whose stories about life along the now lost paths in the Otterburn Ranges we met in an earlier chapter. Geordie Hall:

> My mother would drive geese from Linshiels to Bellingham. She would stay overnight at the Dargues in Redesdale and continue to Bellingham early the next morning.

The first day's walk from Coquetdale, was six miles, starting up the Ridlees Valley, and crossing over the tops and down to Dargues in Redesdale. The next day's walk was seven miles, across the bleak open hills between Redesdale and the North Tyne valley. As geese are usually sent to market just before Christmas, the normal, accepted everyday courage of this woman is impressive. She would have had to deal with the winter weather, whatever it threw up, minding her geese as she went along.

Laurence Pattinson

One story bring us over the Cheviots to Morpeth. Laurence Pattison a retired local carrier, had a story from a friend of his who came from a family of carriers in Harbottle:

> Jimmy Davidson told me that when he was a boy, he would see the drovers coming through the village, over the border from Scotland. They gathered more cattle as they went along. They'd send a lad ahead the day before, so the farmers would get the cattle ready. They'd be identified by earclips. Then they'd walk them to Morpeth market. They were fatstock, going to Morpeth. Jimmy said that it had gone on for hundreds of years.

> They stopped at pubs a lot, so everyone knew them. All the pubs were boarding houses. The drovers would also carry a kind of tent, and poles, on their packhorses. The tent would be sailcloth made waterproof with lanolin or sheep fat, so it would smell strong. The men smelt strong too, as they were working with cattle. Jimmy was in the air force in the war, so we are talking about the twenties and the thirties, and this was still happening.

Sue Rogers

Sometimes, something happens which rises like a vision from the past:

> The other day I met the nearest thing to eighteenth century drovers that you could see in the twenty first century. I was driving my horse trailer towards Alwinton on the little country road from Whittingham, when on the twisty bit above Little Ryle I saw something filling the road ahead so I slowed and then stopped. It was a group of cows and calves plus an enormous bull, all creamily coloured with curly coats, being escorted by four men in suitable ancient garb, two in front and two behind with sticks. No quad bikes or landrovers anywhere. There was a mist over the hills so it was a rather gloomy day and was just like one of those old black and white photographs.

Jonathan Reed

One day in September, I visited Scots Gap mart. Here I found some present day drovers. Several young men and one young woman were darting about, moving the sheep into the pens, into the ring for the sale, and then out the other side to the wagons.

Jonathan Reed spoke to me when things quietened down:

> The job is called 'market drover', but me and the other men, we don't care for the name. It's so old fashioned. My dad did the same job for 50 odd years. Then it was a simple case of putting

the sheep in the pen and moving them in to the auction ring and then out again into the right pen. Nowadays the work is much more skilled. We have to have an NVQ2 in livestock handling, which includes personal safety and hazards to the public, animal welfare and identification of sick animals.

When the sheep arrive in the wagons with their owners, we have to check the licence that each farmer gives us, and make sure that they are bringing the correct number of sheep.

All cattle have a passport which stays with them for life, and every time they come to the mart, the passports go from the farmer to the mart, and from there to whoever purchases them.

There's no droving now like there used to be, although you can still move livestock from one part of your farm to another. In the foot and mouth time, you had to have inspectors from the ministry to supervise it, and they disinfected the road afterwards.

I work part time in Hexham mart, part time at Scots Gap, and two days a week at a dairy farm in Heddon. Also I work in Rothbury mart sometimes, with antiques and furnishings. Thankfully I'm not sitting in front of a computer.

Above left: Jonathan Reed, right, checks lambs being unloaded at Scots Gap mart
Above right: Joe Oliver drives lambs into the pens

Another young lad and a woman were also helping move the sheep from the wagons to the pens, from the pens to the ring, and out again. Joe Oliver in green overalls was kept on the run all through the sale. Libby Bertram wouldn't allow me to take a photo of her, officially, and said No, she wouldn't call herself a drover. Perhaps she could be called a market assistant.

So farmers are still moving their livestock to the markets, where the buyers assemble, though the days of the traditional drovers have ended. From the marts, some of the animals are heading to different farms, to be fattened or for breeding. Others are on their way to the slaughterhouses. From there the carcasses will be driven in motorised vehicles to the supermarkets, and some will be finishing up with the butchers of Morpeth.

Gebhards' butcher shop, Newgate St, 1910

Eddie Gebhard's father John is about 20 years old

The boy is Eddie's Uncle Charles, aged 10

1938

Eddie's father John is 48 years old.

The young woman is Florrie. She lived above the shop.

Photos: from Eddie Gebhard's collection

Dreams of green roads over the hills and country lanes bordered with wild flowers are not what droving is about. The reality is the bringing of animals to market, to be killed, and to provide food for people. The butchers of Morpeth have always been a big part of the life of the town. They still are, even though it is getting harder to produce a good quality product at economic prices, in competition with supermarkets.

After the Second World War, the long distance movement of sheep and cattle to their final destination was by rail, or in motor wagons. Droving short distances still continued for a couple of decades, from the railway station to the mart, from the mart to the overnight fields, and from the mart to the slaughterhouse in the town. As people went about their daily business, it was still a normal thing to see a group of bullocks being driven along the streets.

Everyone who lives in Morpeth knows Gebhards' and Martins', two family shops on Newgate Street. Both are busy, traditional outlets, where the skills of the butchery trade are on full display. They help to complete the story of the drovers, who brought the animals to Morpeth, and ultimately to the dinner plate.

Dennis Martin retired from his shop in 1990. It was always spanking clean, with its smell of bleach as the staff swept the pavement outside, the shining chrome pans exhibiting the newly cut joints in the window. Men in blood-stained overalls carried the carcasses from the delivery wagons across the pavement, in between the passers-by. Dennis had learned the family trade when he was a young boy:

> I worked with my dad in the butchery from when I was 10 or 11 years of age, that would be 1952 or 53. I used to deliver the meat for him, on my bike, until I passed my driving test. I helped in the mart on the Monday, when I was 12 or 13 years old, during the school holidays, and I'd watch the slaughtering.

> Before the war, my dad used to buy cattle at the New Market. The animals would be walked to the slaughter house, along Staithes Lane. That's where the new supermarket is going to be built now. When they were ready, the butchers would go and fetch them in a barrow, or a horse and cart. Nobody bothered much about covering them up, in those days. Now it's all rules and regulations, and health and safety.

> During the war, the meat supply all dried up. It was all rationed. Our family used to get rabbit from a rabbit catcher at Netherwitton. We ate it about twice a week. It was part of our staple diet. You had to eat what you could get.

> My dad was the eldest son of the family, and he ran the shop. He just managed the best he could. My three uncles went to the war. No-one had any money to buy meat in the war.

> The shop was in the same building as Walter Wilson's in Newgate Street. My Uncle Charlie later also had a butcher's shop in Chantry Place. Eventually, the family bought Walter Wilson's and divided the shop in two, the grocery at the front and the butchery being at the rear.

> There used to be a lot of family butchers in the town. In Chantry Place, there were three, Ernie Fail, Tom and Fred Jobson, and Tommy Young. Then there was Vic Rutherford who had a shop on Bridge Street, as well as two on Stobhill and Kirkhill. Dewhirst's was on the Market Place before it moved round the corner. Newgate Street had Gebhards, Stokers, and us. All those butchers would have bought their animals mainly from the mart.

> Some of the cattle which had never been used to people were very wild. When they were brought into the mart, they would dash all over the place, and try to jump out of the ring.

> Cattle used to be kept on Morpeth Common, on land rented by the mart company from the council. They would be walked down High House road to the Mitford road, and then to the mart. Later, when there were wagons, there was a loading bay, off the High House road.

The mart company would buy cattle in Ireland too. The dealer sent them across, and sold them at the mart. We never bought Irish cattle in my shop. They were not fat cattle. They were bought for fattening, and sold later.

When Morpeth slaughterhouse closed in the 1980s, cattle from the mart went to Whitley Bay Meat Company, at Burradon. The carcasses then came to the shop in Newgate Street, and the wagons parked outside.

When we got the carcasses, we did everything in the shop. Nowadays, it's different. Wholesalers buy the meat, and deliver it to many shops in packages, ready prepared. Before, we used to get paid for the bones and fat, but now butchers have to pay for them to be taken away. We used to get paid for skins by the hide companies, but not any more. The slaughtering charges are very high too.

When I was the butcher, I mainly bought at Morpeth mart, but also privately, especially sheep. I'd get them from Chester Hill farm, at Belford, twenty or thirty a week. They'd be delivered in wagons. I also got sheep from the Grahams, at Playing Field Farm in Thropton, and from Mitchell Moore at Tranwell. When we bought the sheep, they'd be killed on the Monday morning, and arrive with us on the Tuesday. They'd do us for the rest of the week.

Eddie Gebhard's family were pork butchers. His grandfather had come from Germany.

We think of Germans as sausage eaters, don't we? There were pork butchers in all the towns round about. There were the Ehrmans in Ashington, Schneiders at Berwick, Hoffmans at Hebburn on Tyneside, and Freddie Lang at Wallsend, who was a relation of my family.

My grandfather died when my father was 17, that would be 1907, so my dad and his sister ran the shop with my grandmother Louisa. They made everything. Black puddings and white puddings, Yorkshire poloney which was a sausage with a red skin; savoury ducks; savaloys which were smoked sausage; hand-raised pork pies – those were the days before moulded pies made in tins; chitterlings which were from the large intestine of the pig. People ate everything in those days, including the offal and tripe. Everything except the squeak, we used to say.

In Germany, the butchers would raise their own pigs. My father had pigs at Cassie Park, near the Oak Inn, through the 30s until the late 40s. At one time, we kept pigs at Longframlington. We did it for 12 years or so, but stopped because we couldn't make it pay. That would be 1968 to 1980.

When I first started the shop, in 1947, all the meat came from the slaughterhouse down Staithes Lane, which was being run by the War Ministry. Each butcher had his own apartment there, and killed the animals himself, or engaged a slaughterman to do it. Then they would take the carcasses to the shop.

Both Eddie Gebhard and Dennis Martin are retired now, but the businesses have been sold on. I think they must still be pleased that their work is enduring.

Lee Belisle is now the owner of Martins'. The shop is still gleaming clean, all the products immaculately presented, the windows and pans sparkling. The busy butchers with their blue-striped aprons are always polite and cheerful, and full of good ideas about how to cook the meat.

Lee started out on a Youth Training Scheme placement, at Walter Wilson's in Amble, 19 years ago. He moved from there to Tommy Wright's butcher's shop at South Broomhill, and from there to Roger Johnson's, who had bought Martin's when Dennis retired. When Roger Johnson was ready to sell, Lee and his partner Geoff Rice raised the finance and took over the business:

Our meat comes from Acklington mart. Bill Howard is our buyer, and he knows exactly what kind of animals to get. He chooses the best Limousin steers and heifers. It costs around £1300 for a good quality steer, a bit less for a heifer. They are bred for lean meat, and that is what our customers want.

The animals then go to Thompsons' abattoir in Witton-le-Wear, in County Durham. They are bought in the mart on Thursday, killed on the Friday or over the weekend, and delivered to me in Morpeth on the Monday.

We buy a lot through the mart from Chris Manners at West Chevington, and from Rentons at High Highlaws, and from Stevensons at Blagdon Burn. A lot of our lambs come from Craig Mellor's farm at Annstead, and from Park Farm near Alnwick which is part of the Northumberland Estates. Also from Findlays at South Carter Moor.

We have a sign in our window saying 'We support local farmers'. We like to buy locally because that is what people are interested in. There is full traceability on all the animals.

Each invoice from the mart shows the identification number of the animals that we buy. You can tell which farm the animals came from, right down to the field where they were grazing. People like their food to be produced locally, but then the prices have to be higher. At the moment, people are less willing to pay higher prices, and it is a struggle. Sometimes people swear at us when we tell them the price. They ask why it is so expensive. They don't want to know about how much we have to pay for the animals, and how much the farmers have to pay for the feedstuffs. But I say, the cheaper you pay, the worse the animal has been treated. Just imagine what a life that chicken had when you can get two for a fiver from the supermarket.

Behind the shop, we do all the preparation. We dry-cure the bacon by rubbing salt into the skin, packing it in a sealed vacuum bag, and letting it mature for a week or more. That Danish bacon you buy is full of water. They cure it by injecting brine into the meat. That's what comes out when you cook it.

The monthly farmers' market makes things harder for us. I don't blame the other competitors. They have to earn a living too. But it was hard on us, very hard, when they changed the day from Sunday to Saturday. No-one is going to buy from the farmers' market and then come to us. Saturday is our main trading day. We have 300 people through the door on Saturdays, and we rely on that day to survive. We and the other traders just thought it was unfair.

The new owners of Gebhards' shop are Sandra and Tony Shaw. Sandra explained how they got into the business in 2009:

We'd started out with rare breed pigs in my brother's woodlands, by the Coquet. We'd got them to help clear out the woodland, and they did a great job. They were Tamworths and Saddlebacks.

Then we got the idea to do hog roasts. We hired a machine, and went round the markets. We started doing parties. The Taylors had bought Gebhards' shop from Eddie, and they used to let us store the carcasses for the hog roasts in their shop. Then when their business came up for sale, we wanted to buy it straight away. It was quite a big thing for us, getting Gebhards'. We were buying into a tradition in Morpeth.

We still do the hog roasts, but we usually use ordinary pigs. They come from Jewitt's in Stanley because the slaughterhouse at Burradon stopped supplying local shops. We changed from the rare breeds because they were not so good. They were more bony with bigger ribs, and fatter. Prices start from £550 for a hog roast party. We just move in and do the feast. If people want organic, we can do that too. We get the pigs from Kielder Organic Farm. Organic pigs start from £700, and most people won't pay that. We also do a drop-off service, which is a third of a pig, and the food that goes with it - everything is home-made.

We don't have a problem with the farmers' market. In fact we used to sell our hog roasts there. It gives local businesses a chance. But it is really hard work. And if the weather is bad, you work at a loss.

Our shop in Morpeth is now called Gebhards Deli Farm Shop. We still specialise in sausages and pies, as well as the bakery. We try to be more of a deli, with sandwiches and soups, and a takeaway service. We are still doing our best to be a traditional Morpeth business.

From at least eight small family butchers' shops in Morpeth in the post-war decades, excluding the supermarkets there are now only Martins' and Gebhards'. In a sign of regeneration perhaps, other butchers are now selling local produce in the Wednesday weekly market and in the monthly farmers' market. This is helping to bring back some of the former character of the town. Jimmy Bell from East Wingates farm is known to everyone as *the Lamb Man*:

> The lamb price collapsed in the end of the 1990s. We knew we had a good product, and we didn't like exporting live lambs to France. We had Texel sheep, prize winners at Acklington mart and Forestburn Gate show. So we made a big decision. We sold the herd of suckler cows, and invested in a butchery, a licensed cutting room and a chilling room. I retrained as a butcher, and Kirsty my wife learned it as well.

> At that time, the Farmers Markets were just starting. I'm now a member of the Farmers' Market committee. We sell nearly all our lambs direct to the customers. I go to eight markets altogether, every month. Every Wednesday to Morpeth, and the first Saturday of every month. The other two are at Tynemouth and Alnwick. I used to go to Ponteland and Hexham, but stopped when they became unprofitable.

> We also sell some lamb via our website. We pack up the meat and despatch it through the Post Office, as they guarantee perishable goods.

> The price of lamb is determined at the auctions. The buyers at the mart compete for the better lambs, and this creates the base price. If the supermarkets offer less than the going rate at the marts, the farmers will not sell to them.

> Our lambs go to the slaughterhouse at Burradon, in North Tyneside. I deliver them in our own truck, and they are returned in chilled vans the next day.

Jimmy Bell, the Lamb Man, with his son John and customers at Morpeth market

On the day I visited him at his farm in Wingates, he and Kirsty were just coming out of their cutting room. "Would you like to have a look round? You're not squeamish are you?" I'm afraid I was. Jimmy said that they've had school children round, who found it fascinating.

Next to Jimmy's stall at the farmers' market was Ian Byatt, of Moorhouse Farm, Stannington. His story was totally different:

> I spent 12 years in the former Soviet Union and eastern Europe, assisting with the changeover from the collective farms to commodity pig production on modern large scale farms. I advised on upgrading the livestock to catch up with improvements in genetics, to help them get food into the shops in the cities. They don't worry about sustainability over there. The people just want to eat.

Animals will only do well if they are treated properly, whether outside or housed in big units. If they don't thrive, they won't grow. If you treat them the right way, they will perform. The quality of the meat depends on how the animals are butchered, and how the meat is hung.

He and his wife Victoria have a farm shop at Stannington a few miles from Morpeth. Their leaflet states: "We have a mixed farm of both livestock and arable. North Country Mule ewes produce quality, well conformed lambs that grow happily on our lowland pasture. We are one of the last farmers rearing pigs in the region. They are grown with high welfare in mind on deep straw in small groups. Our cattle are on grass fields in the summer and are indoors, fed home grown silage and corn, in the winter. We are fortunate to have an excellent abattoir only a few miles from the farm."

As well as two meat stalls at Morpeth's Farmers' Market, there is a poultry stall. James and Sarah Chisholm run *Northumberland Free Range Poultry*, at their Thistleyhaugh farm, by the River Coquet, near Weldon Bridge. And another new stall has opened selling meat from rare breeds at Fontburn.

It is still possible to buy locally produced meat, but this market town does not have a live animal market or a mart anymore. Why is that? We always did in the past, ever since the 1199 charter from King John, the livestock being sold directly in the market place, and the price being negotiated between seller and buyer. At its peak in around 1825, 20,595 cattle and 149,287 lambs, sheep, pigs and calves were sent south from Morpeth.[125]

The story of the closure of the market and the marts is complicated. The booklet, *Morpeth's Market,* is packed full of details about the direct sales in the market place, and the move to the auction marts. The following table contains extracts from the booklet.[126]

1199	King John gave Morpeth its charter to hold a weekly market on Wednesday, which took place in the town centre, in the Market Place.
1858	First auction market, the Morpeth Fat Cattle Mart Company, ran for six years in the Market Place.
1867	Earl of Carlisle (the local lord of the manor) granted Mr Stoll a licence to sell fatstock by auction from a three acre field, on west side of the road to Stobhill, near the railway station. The auctioneer was Sam Donkin.
1887	By this date, 500 sheep and 100 cattle could be accommodated in paved pens at the auction mart near the railway station.
1897	Morpeth Corporation rejected by 13 votes to 2 to move the town centre Market Place location to another site.
1898	The auction mart near the railway station became a company, the Northumberland Farmers' Auction Mart. The shareholders were nearly all local farmers who sent their stock to their own mart. The sale ring was an old black tarred wooden construction covered over by tarpaulin. This same year, a butcher and drover were fined five shillings each for cruelty to stock, and future offenders warned of heavier penalties.
1903	The Corporation opened the Newmarket behind the Town Hall for store cattle (those which needed further fattening), which held 40 pens for 1200 cattle, and an open yard for 200 more. This is roughly where the Leisure Centre is now. Access was through Grey's Yard in Oldgate, but the entrance was narrow.
1905	The Corporation decided to re-start the market for fat cattle (as distinct from store cattle) at the Newmarket. This was the first significant fat cattle market since the arrival of the railway in 1847, which had moved much of the trade to Newcastle. However after some months, this market failed.
1915	Northumberland Farmers' Auction Market bought the three-acre field near the railway station.
1917	An auction was set up in the Newmarket for selling mainly Irish cattle, to try to compete with the success of the Stobhill mart, which had a better location near the railway station.

[125] Edmund Bowman, quoted in Janet Brown, *Morpeth's Market,* p 30
[126] Janet Brown, pp 34 - 45

1917	Wansbeck Farmers' Auction Mart was established on 15 acres of land on the other side of the Stobhill road from the Northumberland Farmers' Mart. So then there were two marts, as well as auctions in the Newmarket.
1920	A dispute arose between Morpeth Corporation and Northumberland Farmers' Mart. It was resolved, among other things, that on Mondays the latter could sell fat cattle on its site near the railway station, but that it could not have weekly sales on Wednesdays.
1924	The Newmarket was made available to all auctioneers on payment of a small fee.
1927	Access to the Newmarket was opened up by demolishing buildings next to the Town Hall. The two station marts used the Newmarket for Wednesday auctions.
1929	Northumberland Farmers' Market and Wansbeck farmers' Auction Mart combined, and became Wansbeck Farmers' Mart.
1939	The Mayor Dick Elliott opened a new mart on the site of the former Wansbeck Farmers' ...s for cattle, pig and calf pens, and ... spacious parking area.
1946	T & I Maughan bought Wansbeck Farmers' Mart.
1957	The last pens were removed from the Newmarket. All sale of live animals was removed to Stobhill. No more animals were sold in the historic centre of Morpeth.

The photo shows the pens in the Newmarket, constructed in 1903. Access was through Grey's Yard in Oldgate. The Town Hall is the building on the centre right, and the building next to it is the Scotch Arms, which was pulled down in 1927.
Photo: Alan Davison collection

Despite the move away from the town centre, the auction marts in Morpeth continued to be an important part of the life of the town, and the work of Morpeth butchers in the second half of the twentieth century. Animals were still brought here, and drovers were still at work.

I visited George Strachan, now 90 years of age, who worked as an auctioneer in Morpeth for T & I Maughan from the early 1950s until he retired in 1985. All the butchers whose stories I've included so far told me to talk to him, saying that there is nothing that he doesn't know about the marts in Morpeth. I asked him to tell me about how the animals came to the market, and any droving stories:

Many of the Irish cattle had started in Dublin market, standing all day long. Then they were put on a ship to Liverpool or Holyhead, and then into railway wagons where they couldn't lie down. Some of them were in bad condition when they arrived in Morpeth, and needed to be seen by the vet. We would put them in sheds, bed them down well with hay, and give them water. Then we would move those that were in good condition the next day. We would walk them to the grass, at Pottery Bank, or the Common. Occasionally we'd take them to Pigdon to Sir William Elliott's farm. He was a director at the mart, and he'd make fields available if we needed extra space.

The animals would be walked through the town centre on the way to Pigdon. It was just a matter of course. The drovers guided them along. Mostly the Irish animals were calm enough. They'd been raised on small farms, and were like family pets. The drovers knew how to drive the animals so as not to upset them. Sometimes if there were 50 or so cattle, they might damage a car. Or the car drivers would get impudent at being kept waiting. Then the drovers would get angry and weren't past threatening with a stick.

They were a bunch of desperadoes in some ways. A good percentage were Scotch or Irish. They would work all day and drink all night, and sleep in the farm buildings.

The auction mart rented fields at the Common, about 75 acres, and I rented fields at Pottery Bank, 19 acres, after 1950, where there was a spring half way up the bank, and we dug it out so the water went into a trough. The animals would be very thirsty. They might have been in the wagons for two days. Also we had the Market Fields, as we called them. They were beyond the mart, where the houses are now.

I used to bring cattle from western of Scotland. I went to the island of Islay every year, for ten years or so, in the 50s and 60s. John Jackson and I would go round the regular farmers. They'd want £100 for the animals which were only worth say £50, and we had to bargain to get the price we wanted. The animals were raised on poor land. They'd be young stock, one to two years old. We'd be buying them for local farmers here in Northumberland. After we bought them, they would be sent on McBrayne's ships to Glasgow, and then by rail to Morpeth. At first they were Aberdeen Angus crosses, but later they'd be Charollais, Simmentals or Limousins. They were fattened in Northumberland.

George Strachan has written a book called *Going, going ....!* from which I've taken the following extract:[127]

When the railways stopped carrying cattle, in the early 1960s, the supply of Irish cattle dried up. We found Fred King from Exeter in Devon who said he could supply us and he used to send a hundred cattle of mixed breeds to Morpeth mart every week. Then Thomas Muckle bought one of the first double-decker cattle wagons in the country. It could hold fifty cattle, and the first time I saw it unloaded I could not believe that it could carry so many animals. We had them delivered to Shadfen farm, near Morpeth, which I was then managing for the Maughans. That meant we had to walk the cattle the two miles to the market, and this could be a nightmare because they were not as quiet as the Irish cattle and often broke ranks into the adjoining fields. With their tails in the air, they would shoot off with us in hot pursuit.

Local people can remember the cattle being driven through the streets of Morpeth when they were still being sold in the Newmarket. Eddie Purdy worked in Bobby Rutherford's barber shop in Bridge Street:

There were cattle pens in the new Market Place by the river then. The Irish men brought the cattle from Ireland, and the bull wallopers brought them down from the station through the street. Everyone put shutters on the shop windows so the cattle wouldn't break the glass. The Irish men came in to get a shave in our shop, and they did their business there. When they completed a bargain, they put a silver coin on their palm, and spat on it, and slapped each other's palm to seal the transaction. They felt really foreign to us. They were hard-working, hard-drinking men.[128]

---

[127] George Strachan, pp 48 - 49
[128] Bridget Gubbins, p 65

The butchers of Morpeth mart
Names supplied by George Strachan
Left to right:
Billy Hayes in cap, looking sideways, butcher from Whitley Bay
Robert Patterson in top hat, butcher from Bedlington
Charles Nicholson, butcher from Whitley Bay
Harold Huntley in cap, butcher from Whitley Bay
Shepherd from Pigdon Farm in cap, name unknown
Jimmy Green, farmer from Linden West Farm, near Morpeth
Ernie Fail in deerstalker, butcher from Morpeth
In cap, at rear, name unknown
George Strachan in white overalls, auctioneer
Ken Gilhespie in no hat, butcher from Blyth
Eddie Fail in trilby, butcher from Blyth
Billy Stainthorpe with glasses, butcher from Tynemouth
John Soulsby on extreme right, butcher from Blyth

Photo: George Strachan collection

William Moore told Morpeth Antiquarian Society a few more stories which Janet Brown recorded in *Morpeth's Market*:

> Bill used to drive his uncle's sheep down the North Road, on the right hand side of the road. In 1913 he was shepherding his flock to Morpeth Market, when a number of animals disappeared into the alley in front of the Beeswing public house. He went in to bring the strays back, but just as he was reaching the street again, a door at the top of the third floor opened and a binful of rubbish was hurled down the stairs, most of it landing over the drover! Thereafter he took sheep down the left side of Newgate Street.

Another time, he was driving a cow along the main street to the Newmarket. … The cow decided to go in at an open door, going up the stairs and into a bedroom. The only way of getting her to descend again was by going under the bed and coming up on the window side of her and driving her out. The owner of the house tried to claim compensation for damage caused but the law was on the side of the cow. If an animal enters an open door, it is the owner's fault for leaving the door open in the first place.[129]

The 1960s to 1980s saw the last days of the mart. Here is the end of its story.

1964	The land of the former Northumberland Farmers' Mart, near the railway station, was sold to build the future Low Stobhill housing estate.
1966	Wansbeck Farmers' Mart was still flourishing. George Strachan was the auctioneer.
1969	The swimming pool, now in the leisure centre, was built on the former Newmarket site
1984	T & I Maughan received an offer for the mart from a Northallerton businessman, and sold it, with a promise that the mart would continue.
1985	The promise was not kept, and Morpeth's mart closed for good.

Janet Brown writes the short, sharp, sad end of the story. "Two developers, Bellways Homes and Leech Homes, have built 79 homes there. So ended Morpeth's long connection with the trade in animals."

Then the drovers went home
Once the drovers had brought the animals to Morpeth, they had to turn around and go home, carrying the proceeds of the sales. Our final words must come from George Robson.

> There were no bills or cheques then tendered for payment, and very little Bank of England paper, the currency being generally private local notes and gold. Guineas instead of sovereigns in my first experience were paid, and I have seen a little table in my father's house covered with spade ace guineas taken in payment at Morpeth.
>
> I have often been asked if we were never attacked by highwaymen, but the palmy days of these gentlemen were over, and although many thousands of pounds were carried along the road from Morpeth by Wooler to Scotland in this way, I never yet heard of the least attempt at robbery on the road.
>
> Many of the drovers and market people had to make return journeys on foot, of 15, 21 and 33 miles after a fatiguing day at the market. I remember travelling 33 miles to my bed at Bender every Wednesday after market between November and May, over Rimside Moor, often half-way to the knees in snow … If we did not reach our destination before midnight, sleep was sure to overtake us … We were of course walking in company with others, and suddenly we found ourselves standing bolt upright, probably a hundred yards or so behind our comrades. This would occur twice or thrice in a mile, and then we were all right again.

We've accompanied them on their droving routes, and so we know that they might have found their beds at Mrs Wardle's inn on Rimside Moor which was 15 miles from Morpeth; or at any of the hostelries of Whittingham, Glanton and Powburn at about 21 miles; or as far as the Black Bull at Bendor which was 33 miles away. They would arrive at their beds either very late on Wednesday or in the early hours of Thursday morning.

They would have a day's rest if they were lucky, because on the Friday they would collect the next batch of animals, and soon, they would be droving again to Morpeth town.

---

[129] Janet Brown, pp 35 - 36

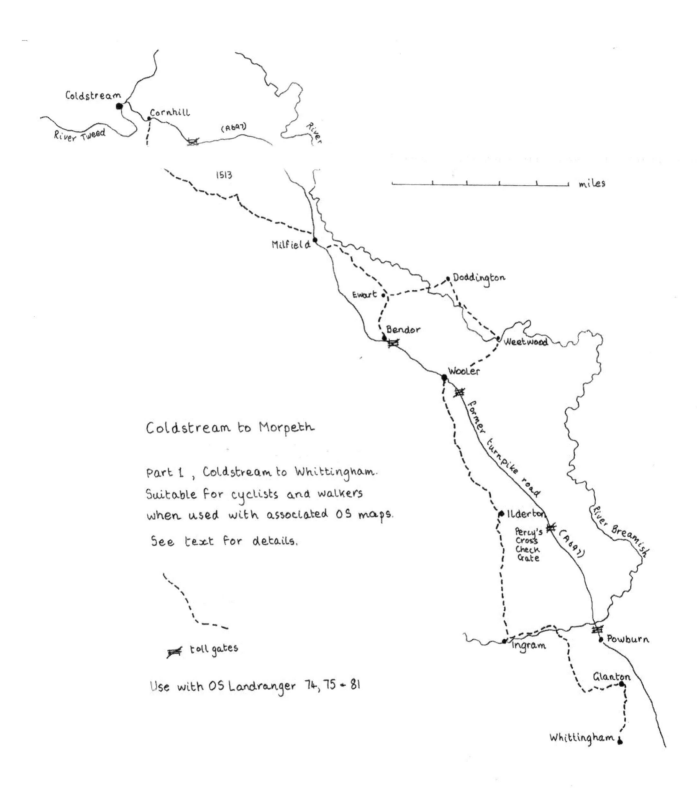

Coldstream to Morpeth

Part 1 , Coldstream to Whittingham.
Suitable for cyclists and walkers
when used with associated OS maps.

See text for details.

⚏ toll gates

Use with OS Landranger 74, 75 & 81

Appendix – Map for Chapter 3, part 2

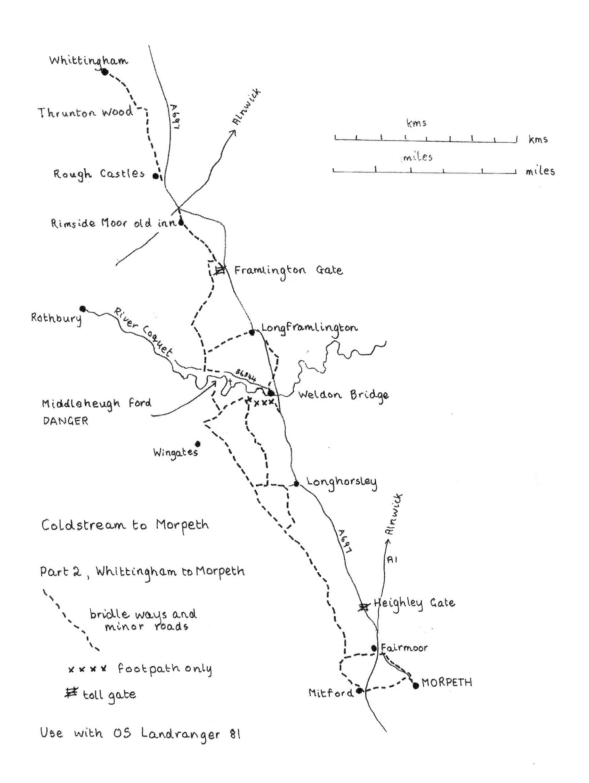

Whittingham

Thrunton Wood

Rough Castles

A697

Alnwick

kms
kms
miles
miles

Rimside Moor old inn

Framlington Gate

Rothbury

River Coquet

Longframlington

B6344

Weldon Bridge

Middleheugh ford
DANGER

x x x

Wingates

Longhorsley

A697

Alnwick

A1

Coldstream to Morpeth

Part 2, Whittingham to Morpeth

Heighley Gate

bridle ways and
minor roads

Fairmoor

x x x x footpath only

MORPETH

⌗ toll gate

Mitford

Use with OS Landranger 81

Appendix - Map for Chapter 5, part 1

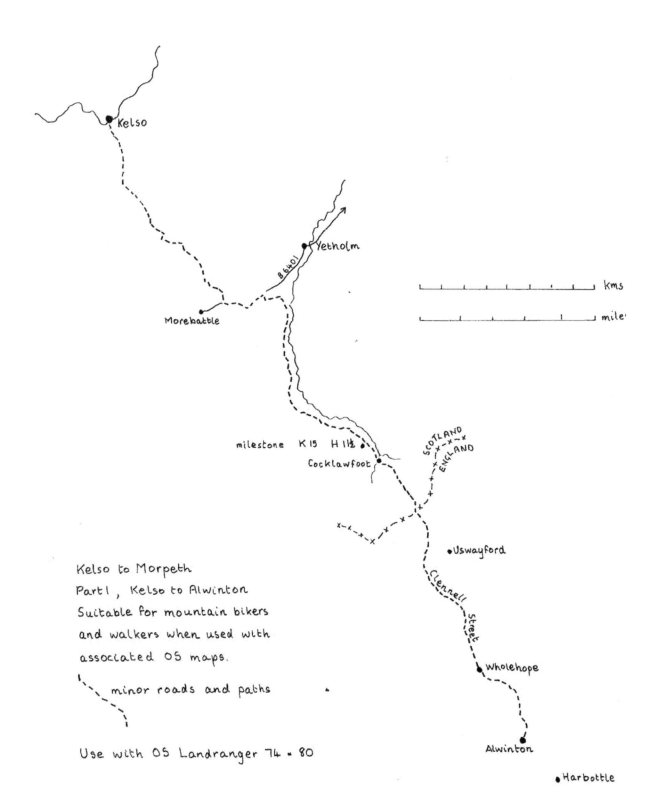

Kelso

Yetholm

B6401

Morebattle

kms

mile

milestone K 15 H 1½

Cocklawfoot

SCOTLAND
x—x—x
ENGLAND

x—x—x—x—x

Uswayford

Clennell Street

Kelso to Morpeth
Part I , Kelso to Alwinton
Suitable for mountain bikers
and walkers when used with
associated OS maps.

minor roads and paths

Wholehope

Alwinton

Harbottle

Use with OS Landranger 74 - 80

116

Appendix – Map for Chapter 5, part 2, and Chapter 5A

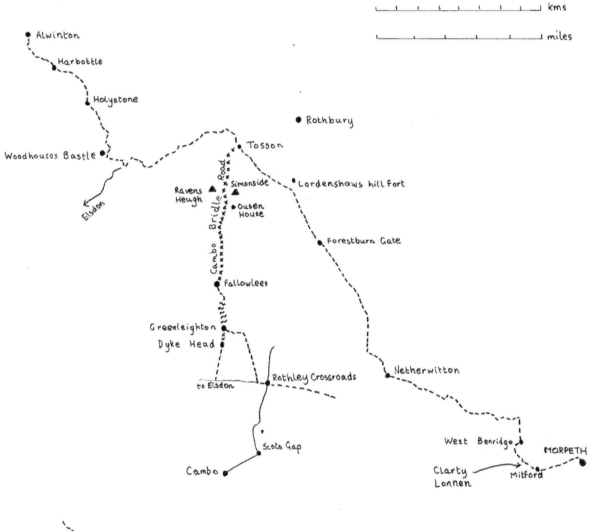

Kelso to Morpeth
Part 2 , Alwinton to Morpeth
and
Cambo Bridle Road
Use with Landranger 81

kms

miles

Alwinton

Harbottle

Holystone

Rothbury

Woodhouses Bastle

Tosson

Elsdon

Simonside

Lordenshaws hill Fort

Ravens Heugh

Ousen House

Forestburn Gate

Cambo Bridle Road

Fallowlees

Greenleighton

Dyke Head

Netherwitton

to Elsdon

Rothley Crossroads

Scots Gap

West Benridge

MORPETH

Cambo

Clarty Lonnen

Mitford

- - - - - minor roads suitable for cyclists and walkers

x x x x footpath for walkers only

path on Access Land, not marked on all maps

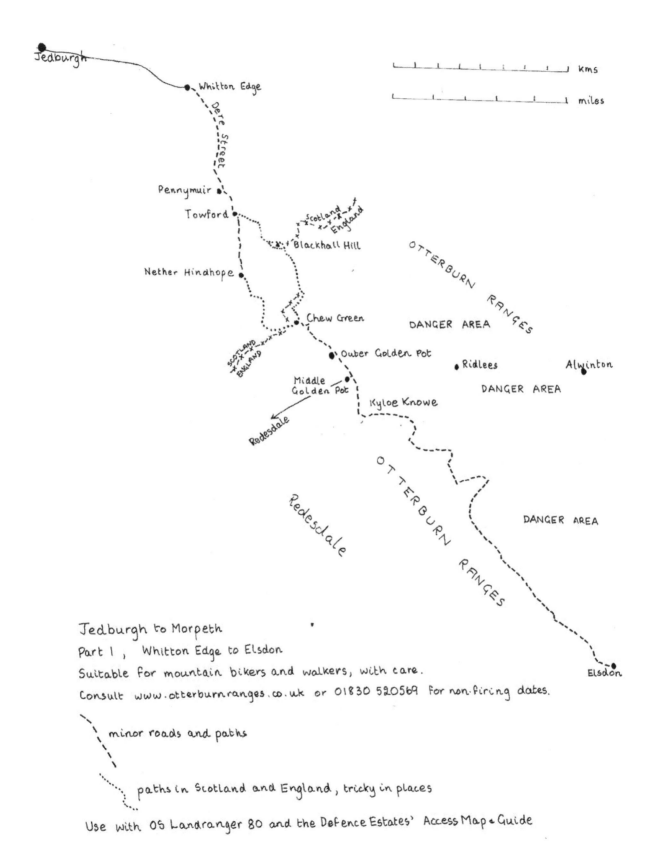

Jedburgh to Morpeth
Part 1 , Whitton Edge to Elsdon
Suitable for mountain bikers and walkers, with care.
Consult www.otterburnranges.co.uk or 01830 520569 for non-firing dates.

- - - minor roads and paths

······ paths in Scotland and England, tricky in places

Use with OS Landranger 80 and the Defence Estates' Access Map & Guide

Appendix – Map for Chapter 7, part 2

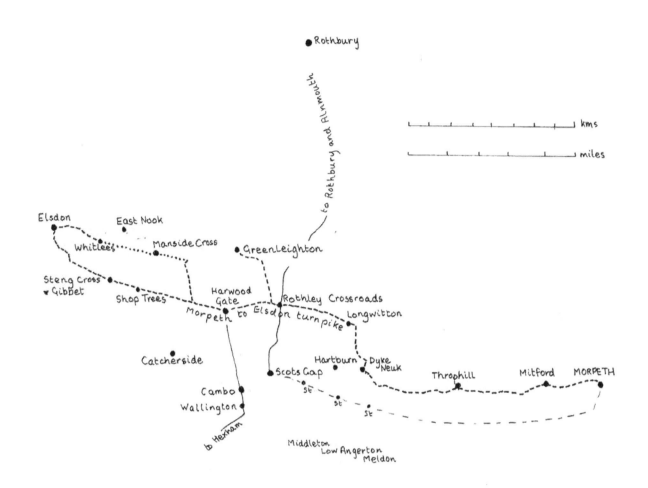

Jedburgh to Morpeth
Part 2 , Elsdon to Morpeth
Suitable for cyclists and walkers.

‑‑‑‑ minor roads and bridle ways

‑‑‑‑ footpaths

‑ ‑ ‑ st ‑ ‑ ‑ former railway line and station

Use with OS Landranger 80 + 81

Bibliography

Albert, William, *The Turnpike Road System in England 1663 – 1840,* Cambridge 1972

Anderson, George Murray, *From the Glens to the Lowlands,* New Horizons, 1979

Bailey, J, Culley, G, *General View of the Agriculture of Northumberland, Cumberland and Westmorland,* first published 1794, this edition facsimile of third edition 1805, Frank Graham, 1972

Bogg, Edmund, *A Thousand Miles of Wandering in the Border Country*, Mawson Swan and Morgan, 1898

Beckensall, Stan, *Prehistoric Rock Art in Northumberland*, Tempus, 2001

Bogle, Kenneth R, *Scotland's Common Ridings*, Tempus, 2004

Bonser, K J, *The Drovers,* Macmillan, 1970, this edition Country Book Club, 1972

Bosanquet, Rosalie, ed, *In the Troublesome Times,* 1929, reprinted 1989 by The Spredden Press

Brown, Janet, ed, *Morpeth's Market,* Morpeth Antiquarian Society, 1999

Brewis, William, *The Diaries of William Brewis of Mitford, 1833-1850*, ed Hilary Kristensen, 2007, Wagtail Press

Bridges and Roads Committee minutes, Northumberland County Council, 1949 – 1960, at Northumberland Archives

Burt, Edward, *Letters Concerning Scotland,* first published 1754. This selection from *Beyond the Highland Line,* edited A J Youngson, Collins, 1974

Carlton, Richard, *The Anglo-Scottish Border Roads of the Cheviot Hills,* Northumberland National Park, 2009

Commons Open Spaces and Footpaths Society, *Surveys and Maps of Public Rights of Way,* 1950

Cowper, R A S, *Journal of the Newcastle upon Tyne Agricultural Society,* 1970 – 71, vol 24

Dixon, David Dippie, *Whittingham Vale,* first published 1895, this edition Frank Graham, 1979; *Upper Coquetdale*, first published 1903, this edition Frank Graham 1974

Dodds, W G, *The Turnpike Trusts of Northumberland*, MA thesis, University of Durham, 1965, at Northumberland Archives

Fraser, George McDonal, *Steel Bonnets,* Pan, 1971

Frodsham, Paul, *In the Valley of the Sacred Mountain,* Northern Heritage Publishing, 2006

Gubbins, Bridget, *The Curious Yards and Alleyways of Morpeth,* Greater Morpeth Development Trust, 2011

Haldane, A R B, *The Drove Roads of Scotland,* 1952, this edition David & Charles, 1973

Lancaster University Archaeological Unit, *Simonside Archaeological Landscape Project,* Northumberland National Park, 2000

Mackay, John James, *Border Highways,* self published, 1998

Mackenzie, E, *A Historical and Descriptive View of the County of Northumberland*, Vols I and 2, Mackenzie and Dent, 1811

Moffat, Alistair, *The Reivers,* 2009, Birlinn

Mundell, Matt, *Country Diary,* Gordon Wright, 1991

Northumberland Education Committee, *Northumberland, England's Farthest North,* 1953

Owen, S F, *Coquetdale Camera: The Photographs of W P Collier,* Bellingham Heritage Centre, 2005

Parson W M and White Wm, *History, Directory and Gazetteer of the Counties of Durham and Northumberland,* 1828

Philipson, John, *Wanderers from Westminster,* from *Clippings* Upper Coquetdale Publications, 1989

Purves, Andrew, *A Shepherd Remembers*, Tuckwell Press, 2001

Riddall, John, Trevelyan, John, *Rights of Way: A guide to law and practice,* Commons, Open Spaces and Footpaths Preservation Society and Ramblers Association, 1992

Roberts Ian, Carlton, Richard, Rushworth, Alan, *Drove Roads of Northumberland,* The History Press, 2010

Robson, Robert, *Bob's Bridges,* Northumberland County Council and others, 1998, p 66

Rowland, Harry, *The Alemouth or Corn Road,* self-published, undated but about 1980

Scott, Sir Walter, *The Two Drovers,* 1827, this edition Penguin Classics, 2003; *Rob Roy,* 1817, this edition Everyman 1995

Stevenson, Robert Louis, *St Ives,* 1897, William Heineman, this edition Richard Drew, 1990

Strachan, George, *Going, going ...!* self-published, 2007

Surtees, Robert, *Hillingdon Hall,* 1845, this edition Nonesuch Publishing, 2006

Thompson, William, *Cattle Droving between Scotland and England,* Journal of the British Archaeological Association, 1932

Trevelyan, Sir Charles, *Wallington, Its History and Treasures,* self-published, 1950

Tweddle, A H, *Town Trails for Morpethians,* no 1, 1980, re-published by Davison and Harle, Northumberland County Library Service, 2007

Whitaker, Harold, *A descriptive list of the maps of Northumberland by Harold Whitaker,* Society of Antiquaries of Newcastle upon Tyne, 1949

Alan Young, Alan, *Railways in Northumberland,* Martin Bairstow, 2003

Ilustrations
Coldstream Bridge, by J H A Selgrave, from Edmund Bogg's *A Thousand Miles of Wandering in the Border Country*, 1898, p 201

Road at High Rochester, a sketch by the Duchess of Northumberland sculpted by F C Lewis, from Hodgson's *History of Northumberland*, 1827, Part II, Vol I, p 149

Hole in the Wall, Whittingham, by J Turnbull Dixon, from David Dippie Dixon's *Whittingham Vale*, 1895, p 181

Brinkburn Priory, by C J Bigge and W Collard, from Hodgson's *History of Northumberland*, 1840, part II Vol III, inside the back cover

Reivers, by Gilbert Foster, from Edmund Bogg's *A Thousand Miles of Wandering in the Border Country,* 1898, p225

Bastle, by F C Lewis, from Hodgson's *History of Northumberland*, 1835, Part III Vol III, inside the back cover

Percy's Cross, by an un-named artist, from Edmund Bogg's *A Thousand Miles of Wandering in the Border Country*, p 186

Shepherd reading, by P M Teasdale, from Edmund Bogg's *A Thousand Miles of Wandering in the Border Country*, 1898, p 271

Unacknowledged photos, maps and drawings are by the author

Documents at Northumberland Archives

Northumberland - General Quarter Sessions of the Peace held at Morpeth the 13th of January 1686, QSO 1/263

George Robson, *The Old Cattle Market at Morpeth. A Old Northumbrian's Recollections*, SANT/BEQ/28/1/12 Also *Morpeth: Its Cattle Market and its Inns*

Plan of the Town and Part of the Borough of Morpeth, 1852, NRO 5789

Commons Report on Morpeth and Edinburgh Road, 1822, NRO 530.15/63. Includes Thomas Telford's survey

James Cunningham, Map Present and Proposed Lines of Road from POWBURN to WELDON BRIDGE", 1831, QRU/26

Longframlington Township Tithe Award 1843, EP 12/51

Turnpike file at Northumbrian Archives, *Composite lists of Turnpike, Manorial and Electoral Material*

Tosson or Hepple Enclosure Plan and Award, 1806 – 1807, QRA 51/1

Elsdon Tithe Map, 1839, DT 164-4M

Ford and Lowick turnpike renewal act 1812, George III, Q/R/UP/7

Documents at Newcastle Library Local Studies, L 625.7

Morpeth to Elsdon turnpike act 1751, George II

Longhorsley to Percy's Cross turnpike act 1751, George II

Ford and Lowick turnpike act 1792, George III

Percy's Cross to Milfield Burn turnpike act 1807, George III

Percy's Cross to Milfield Burn turnpike act 1808, George III

Ford and Lowick turnpike renewal act 1812, George III, Q/R/UP/7 (Northumberland Archives)

General turnpike act 1822, George IV

Longhorsley to Percy's Cross turnpike renewal act 1820, George IV

Percy's Cross to Milfield Burn turnpike renewal act 1829, George IV

Maps and tapes at Northumberland Archives

Armstrong's maps of Northumberland, 1769

Fryer's maps of Northumberland, 1820

Greenwood's maps of Northumberland, 1828

First edition Ordnance Survey maps, 1860s

Second edition Ordnance Survey maps, 1890s

George Murray, NRO T/62 and NRO T/63

Eddie Bertram, NRO T/127